Student Activities Manual

Disce!

An Introductory Latin Course

Kenneth F. Kitchell, Jr.
University of Massachusetts Amherst

Thomas J. Sienkewicz
Monmouth College

Historical Consultant: Gregory Daugherty
Randolph Macon College

Prentice Hall
Boston Columbus Indianapolis
New York San Francisco Upper Saddle River
Amsterdam Cape Town Dubai London
Madrid Milan Munich Paris Montréal Toronto
Delhi Mexico City São Paulo Sydney
Hong Kong Seoul Singapore Taipei Tokyo

Executive Acquisitions Editor: Rachel McCoy
Editorial Assistant: Noha Amer Mahmoud
Executive Marketing Manager: Kris Ellis-Levy
Marketing Coordinator: William J. Bliss
Senior Managing Editor for Product Development: Mary Rottino
Associate Managing Editor: Janice Stangel
Production Project Manager: Manuel Echevarria
Project Manager: Assunta Petrone, Preparé, Italy
Audio-Visual Project Manager: Gail Cocker
Development Editor for Assessment: Melissa Marolla Brown

Media Editor: Meriel Martínez
Executive Editor, MyLanguageLabs: Bob Hemmer
Senior Media Editor: Samantha Alducin
Senior Art Director: Pat Smythe
Interior/cover Designer: Wanda España
Cartographer: Peter Bull Art Studio
Line Art Studio: Peter Bull Art Studio
Senior Manufacturing and Operations Manager, Arts and Sciences: Nick Sklitsis
Operations Specialist: Cathleen Petersen
Publisher: Phil Miller

Cover image: ML Sinibaldi/CORBIS

This book was set in 11/14 Times New Roman.

22 2023

Prentice Hall
is an imprint of

Student Activities Manual for Disce! Volume 1

ISBN 10:
0-13-612626-X

ISBN 13:
978-0-13-612626-3

www.pearsonhighered.com

Contents

1 Intrōductiō

01-01 *Familia Servīliī.* Identify the character from Servilius' family described in the first sentence. Select that person's name from the *Thēsaurus Nominum* and insert it in the second sentence. Some of the names may be used more than once. Follow the model.

Thēsaurus Nominum

Avus	Marcus Servīlius Sevērus
Caecilia Metella Secunda	Marcus Servīlius Sevērus M.f.
Lūcius Servīlius Noniānus	Servīlia

→ I am the current wife of Servilius. *Quid nōmen mihi est?* (What is my name?)

   Nōmen mihi <u>Caecilia Metella Secunda</u> est. (My name is _____)

1. I am the head of the upper-class family.

   Nōmen mihi _____ *est.*

2. I am a 16-year-old girl in an upper-class Roman family.

   Nōmen mihi _____ *est.*

3. My stepbrother is Marcus.

   Nōmen mihi _____ *est.*

4. My husband is Servilius.

   Nōmen mihi _____ *est.*

5. M. Servīlius Sevērus is my son.

   Nōmen mihi _____ *est.*

6. Servilia and I have the same mother.

   Nōmen mihi _____ *est.*

7. I am running for the office of praetor.

   Nōmen mihi _____ *est.*

01-02 *Familia Valeriae.* Identify the character from Valeria's family described in the first sentence. Select that person's name from the *Thēsaurus Nominum* and insert it in the second sentence. Some of the names may be used more than once. Follow the model.

Thēsaurus Nominum

Flāvia	Marcus Aelius
Gāius Licinius C.f.	Plōtia
Licinia	Sōcratēs
	Valeria

→ My husband is Aelius. *Quid nōmen mihi est?*
  Nōmen mihi _____ **Licinia** _____ est.

1. I am a 40-year-old widow.
   Nōmen mihi _____ *est.*

2. I am German.
   Nōmen mihi _____ *est.*

3. My wife is Licinia.
   Nōmen mihi _____ *est.*

4. I moved to Rome after the death of my husband Licinius a few years ago.
   Nōmen mihi _____ *est.*

5. I am the pet monkey of the Licinia family.
   Nōmen mihi _____ *est.*

6. I am Valeria's son.
   Nōmen mihi _____ *est.*

7. My daughter is Valeria.
   Nōmen mihi _____ *est.*

8. I am pregnant.
   Nōmen mihi _____ *est.*

01-03 *Familia Valeriae.* Select all the members of Valeria's household living in Rome.

_____ C. Licinius C.f.

_____ Caecilia Metella Secunda

_____ Flāvia

_____ Licinia

_____ Lūcius Servīlius Noniānus

_____ Marcus Aelius

_____ Marcus Servīlius Sevērus

_____ Marcus Servīlius Sevērus M.f.

_____ Plōtia

_____ Servīlia

_____ Sōcratēs

_____ Valeria

Name: _____   **Date:** _____

01-04 *Familia Servīliī.* Select all the members of Servilius' household.

_____ Avus

_____ C. Licinius C.f.

_____ Caecilia Metella Secunda

_____ Flāvia

_____ Gāius Licinius C.f.

_____ Licinia

_____ Lūcius Servīlius Noniānus

_____ Marcus Aelius

_____ Marcus Servīlius Sevērus

_____ Marcus Servīlius Sevērus M.f.

_____ Servīlia

_____ Sōcratēs

_____ Valeria

01-05 Rules for Pronouncing Latin. Indicate whether each of the following statements is true or false.

1. There are no silent letters in Latin.   T   F

2. Latin is inconsistent in the sound a letter represents.   T   F

3. The majority of Latin consonants are pronounced much as they are in English.   T   F

4. There is no letter "J" in classical Latin.   T   F

5. The letter "C" is pronounced in Latin as in the English word "receive."   T   F

6. Two vowels creating a single sound are called a diphthong.   T   F

7. The last syllable of a two-syllable word is always stressed in Latin.   T   F

8. Latin always stresses the first syllable of a two-syllable word.   T   F

9. The next-to-last syllable of a Latin word is called the penult.   T   F

10. A Latin word has as many syllables as it has vowels or diphthongs.   T   F

01-06 Some Important Terms. Match each word with its meaning.

1. penult _____   **a.** a long mark placed over a long vowel

2. antepenult _____   **b.** two vowels creating a single sound

3. diphthong _____   **c.** the last syllable of a Latin word

4. inscription _____   **d.** the next-to-last syllable of a Latin word

5. ultima _____   **e.** the syllable before the next-to-last syllable of a Latin word

6. macron _____   **f.** writing carved onto buildings and other stone objects

01-07 How Many Syllables? Select the choice that indicates the number of syllables in each Latin word.

1. ambulat	1	2	3	4
2. fēmina	1	2	3	4
3. filiābus	1	2	3	4
4. mihi	1	2	3	4
5. Rōmānōrum	1	2	3	4
6. quaenam	1	2	3	4
7. quās	1	2	3	4
8. potuimus	1	2	3	4

01-08 Syllables in Latin Words. Select the choice that shows how the Latin word should be broken into syllables.

1. factus	**a.** fact-us	**b.** fac-tus	
2. bonae	**a.** bon-ae	**b.** bo-nae	**c.** bo-na-e
3. abiēs	**a.** a-bi-ēs	**b.** ab-iēs	**c.** abi-ēs
4. pōculīs	**a.** pō-cu-līs	**b.** pōc-ul-īs	**c.** pōc-ulīs
5. speciēbus	**a.** spe-ci-ē-bus	**b.** speci-ē-bus	**c.** spec-iē-bus
6. termina	**a.** term-in-a	**b.** ter-min-a	**c.** ter-mi-na
7. ferāmus	**a.** fer-āmus	**b.** ferā-mus	**c.** fe-rā-mus

01-09 Pronunciation. The following words were taken directly from Latin into English. Indicate the syllable on which the stress falls in Latin by selecting: S3, S2, or S1. Be careful—some words came into English with the same stress, some did not.

1. ēducātor	S3	S2	S1
2. gladiātor	S3	S2	S1
3. rabiēs	S3	S2	S1
4. ōrātor	S3	S2	S1
5. specimen	S3	S2	S1
6. ignōrāmus	S3	S2	S1
7. lēgislātor	S3	S2	S1
8. ulterior	S3	S2	S1
9. vacuum	S3	S2	S1
10. videō	S3	S2	S1

01-10 Working with Pronunciation. Select the English word that reflects the way the Latin letter is pronounced.

1. Latin V sounds like:

    a. **v**estibule   **b.** **w**ore   **c.** di**v**est

2. Latin C sounds like:

    a. ni**c**e   **b.** **c**ease   **c.** **c**ut

3. The Latin consonant blend GN sounds like:

    a. lu**g n**ut   **b.** lasa**gn**a   **c.** zi**ng**

4. The Latin consonant blend TH sounds like:

    a. wor**th**   **b.** pen**th**ouse   **c.** **th**ese

5. The Latin G sounds like:

    a. **g**ood   **b.** sa**g**e   **c.** **g**eometry

6. Long E (*ē*) sounds like:

    a. t**ea**m   **b.** s**e**t   **c.** w**eigh**

7. Long U (*ū*) sounds like:

    a. b**oo**t   **b.** d**u**ck   **c.** **u**niversal

8. The Latin diphthong *ae* sounds like:

    a. **ai**sle   **b.** p**a**triot   **c.** p**a**tty

9. The Latin diphthong *oe* sounds like:

    a. Ph**oe**nix   **b.** b**oi**l   **c.** N**oe**l

10. Latin QU sounds like:

    a. **qu**est   **b.** tor**que**   **c.** **k**ey

01-11 Parts of Speech: Verbs. Select all the verbs you see in this brief paragraph. If any are repeated, select them each time they appear.

> Valeria and Licinia work hard at the shop. They serve wine and bread to hungry and thirsty customers during the day. The customers pay with small coins and often leave a tip for Licinia. She is happy and greatly appreciates it.

01-12 Parts of Speech: Nouns. Select all the nouns you see in this brief paragraph. If any are repeated, select them each time they appear.

> Valeria and Licinia work hard at the shop. They serve wine and bread to hungry and thirsty customers during the day. The customers pay with small coins and often leave a tip for Licinia. She is happy and greatly appreciates it, but does not expect it.

01-13 Parts of Speech: Pronouns. Select all the pronouns you see in this brief paragraph. If any are repeated, select them each time they appear.

> Valeria and Licinia work hard at the shop. They serve wine and bread to hungry and thirsty customers during the day. The customers pay with small coins and often leave a tip for Licinia. She is happy and greatly appreciates it, but does not expect it.

01-14 Parts of Speech: Prepositions. Select all the prepositions you see in this brief paragraph. If any are repeated, select them each time they appear.

> Valeria and Licinia work hard at the shop. They serve wine and bread to hungry and thirsty customers during the day. The customers pay with small coins and often leave a tip for Licinia. She is happy and greatly appreciates it, but does not expect it.

01-15 Parts of Speech: Conjunctions. Select all the conjunctions you see in this brief paragraph. If any are repeated, select them each time they appear.

> Valeria and Licinia work hard at the shop. They serve wine and bread to hungry and thirsty customers during the day. The customers pay with small coins and often leave a tip for Licinia. She is happy and greatly appreciates it, but does not expect it.

01-16 Parts of Speech: Adjectives. Select all the adjectives you see in this brief paragraph. If any are repeated, select them each time they appear.

> Valeria and Licinia work hard at the shop. They serve wine and bread to hungry and thirsty customers during the day. The customers pay with small coins and often leave a tip for Licinia. She is happy and greatly appreciates it, but does not expect it.

01-17 Parts of Speech. Identify the part of speech of each of the following Latin words. The English meanings are in parentheses.

1. *ambulat* (walks)

| noun | verb | adjective | pronoun | preposition |

2. *in* (in, on)

| noun | verb | adjective | pronoun | preposition |

3. *vir* (man)

| noun | verb | adjective | pronoun | preposition |

4. *bona* (good)

| noun | verb | adjective | pronoun | preposition |

5. *fēmina* (woman)

| noun | verb | adjective | pronoun | preposition |

6. *respondet* (respond)

| conjunction | verb | adjective | pronoun | preposition |

7. *et* (and)

| conjunction | interjection | adjective | pronoun | preposition |

8. *meum* (my)

| conjunction | interjection | adjective | pronoun | preposition |

9. *Ō!* (Oh!)

| conjunction | interjection | adjective | pronoun | preposition |

10. *mē* (me)

| conjunction | interjection | adjective | pronoun | adverb |

11. *lentē* (slowly)

| conjunction | interjection | adjective | pronoun | adverb |

01-18 *Verba Discenda.* Select the correct part of speech for each *verbum discendum.*

1. *est*   pronoun   noun   verb
2. *mihi*   pronoun   noun   verb
3. *nōmen*   pronoun   noun   verb
4. *quid*   pronoun   noun   verb
5. *tibi*   pronoun   noun   verb

01-19 *Verba Discenda.* Select the *verbum discendum* that corresponds to the English words.

1. to me, my: *est*   *mihi*   *nōmen*   *quid*   *tibi*
2. is: *est*   *mihi*   *nōmen*   *quid*   *tibi*
3. what: *est*   *mihi*   *nōmen*   *quid*   *tibi*
4. to you, your: *est*   *mihi*   *nōmen*   *quid*   *tibi*
5. name: *est*   *mihi*   *nōmen*   *quid*   *tibi*

01-20 Translating Latin. Use the *Verba Ūtenda* provided to choose the correct translation of each Latin sentence. Words marked in **bold** are Verba Discenda.

VERBA ŪTENDA		
ambulat walks	***est* is**	***quid* what?**
clāmat shouts	*fēmina* woman	*respondet* responds
currit runs	*fīlia* daughter	*stat* stands
dat gives	*fīlius* son	***tibi* your, to you**
dīcit speaks	***mihi* my, to me**	*vendit* sells
dūcit leads	***nōmen, -inis* n. name**	*vir* man

1. *Fēmina dīcit.*
   a. The woman speaks.   **b.** The woman leads.   **c.** The woman runs.
2. *Fēmina dūcit.*
   a. The woman speaks.   **b.** The woman leads.   **c.** The woman runs.
3. *Fīlius currit.*
   a. The son leads.   **b.** The son shouts.   **c.** The daughter runs.   **d.** The son runs.
4. *Fīlia vendit.*
   a. The daughter runs.   **b.** The son shouts.   **c.** The daughter sells.   **d.** The daughter leads.
5. *Vir ambulat.*
   a. The man runs.   **b.** The man walks.   **c.** The man shouts.   **d.** The man leads.

01-21 How Closely Did You Read? Use the *Thēsaurus Verbōrum* to fill in the blanks.

Thēsaurus Verbōrum

Arch of Titus	Judaea	*Servīliī*
Caecilia	Licinia	Valeria
Festīnā lentē!	Marcus	
harēna	S.P.Q.R.	

1. The emperor Vespasian sent his son Titus to suppress the revolt in this province: _____
2. Make haste slowly!: _____
3. The wife of Servilius: _____
4. Refers to "The Senate and the Roman People": _____
5. The upper-class family in the story: _____
6. This word means "sand" in Latin and a sporting facility in English: _____
7. The woman who runs a snack shop with her daughter: _____
8. Monument erected to celebrate a Roman military victory: _____
9. Lucius' older brother: _____
10. She is the married daughter in the lower-class family: _____

01-22 Crossword Puzzle. Complete the puzzle with information from the chapter.

Across

1 – Father of Marcus
2 – Wife of Servilius
4 – Son of Caecilia
5 – German slave who works for Valeria
8 – Augustus' personal motto
12 – Next to last syllable in a Latin word
13 – Runs a snack shop
15 – Third syllable from the end in a Latin word
16 – Valeria's son-in-law
17 – Brother of Lucius

Down

1 – 16-year-old daughter of Servilius
3 – Valeria's son, serving in Germany
6 – Valeria's daughter
7 – Two vowels pronounced as one sound
9 – Servilia's grandfather
10 – Pet monkey of the snack shop
11 – Last syllable in a Latin word
12 – Licinia's grandmother
14 – Abbreviation found on many Roman buildings

2   In Tabernā

02-01 Comprehension Exercise on *Lectiō Prīma*. Use this picture from *Lectiō Prīma* to complete the following sentences. Follow the model.

Valeria   **Licinia**   **Flavia**

→ *Valeria* ad sinistram est.

1. _____ ancilla est.

2. _____ domina est.

3. _____ māter est.

4. _____ fīlia est.

5. _____ Germānica est.

02-02 Recognizing Number. Indicate whether each verb is singular or plural. HINT: The personal endings *-t* and *-nt* will help you.

1. *est*   singular   plural

2. *sunt*   singular   plural

3. *vendit*   singular   plural

4. *vendunt*   singular   plural

5. *ambulant*   singular   plural

6. *ambulat*   singular   plural

7. *videt*   singular   plural

02-03 Recognizing Number. Select all the plural verbs from the following list.

_____ bibunt   _____ dat

_____ vident   _____ venit

_____ bibit   _____ dant

_____ veniunt   _____ inquit

02-04 Recognizing Derivatives in *Lectiō Prīma*. List as many English derivatives as you can for each of the Latin words from *Lectiō Prīma*. Follow the model. If you need help finding derivatives, use an English dictionary.

→ pictūrā   *picture, pictorial, picturesque*

1. domina   _____
2. fēminae   _____
3. fīlia   _____
4. sinistram   _____
5. tabernā   _____
6. vendit   _____
7. ancilla   _____

02-05 Recognizing Subjects and Their Verbs. Select the subject and the verb in each sentence. Where there are multiple verbs or subjects, select them all.

1. In pictūrā trēs fēminae sunt.
2. Fēmina ad sinistram Valeria est.
3. Valeria Itala est.
4. Fēmina prope Valeriam Licinia est.
5. Valeria est māter et Licinia fīlia est.
6. Flāvia ancilla est et Valeria domina est.
7. In tabernā Valeria pōtum et cibum vendit.

02-06 Identifying Subjects and Verbs. Identify the bold words in the following sentences as subject, verb, or neither.

1. *Fēmina in tabernā **est**.*
     a. subject   **b.** verb   **c.** neither

2. *Fēmina prope **Valeriam** Licinia est.*
     a. subject   **b.** verb   **c.** neither

3. ***Valeria** pōtum vendit.*
     a. subject   **b.** verb   **c.** neither

4. *Flāvia Germānica in **tabernā** est.*
     a. subject   **b.** verb   **c.** neither

5. *Trēs **fēminae** in pictūrā sunt.*
     a. subject   **b.** verb   **c.** neither

6. *Valeria in tabernā **labōrat** (works).*
     a. subject   **b.** verb   **c.** neither

7. *Valeria et **Licinia** in tabernā labōrant.*
     a. subject   **b.** verb   **c.** neither

02-07 Translating the Present Tense: Aspect. Translate each verb three ways. Follow the model.

→ *ambulant* (walk)   they walk, they do walk, they are walking

1. *bibit* (drink)   _____

2. *vendit* (sell)   _____

3. *dant* (give)   _____

4. *respondet* (answer) _____

5. *respondent* (answer) _____

02-08 Recognizing Verb Forms. Select all the verb forms that are a 1st principal part.

_____ ambulāre

_____ bibō

_____ bibere

_____ dō

_____ dare

_____ venīre

_____ veniō

02-09 Recognizing Verb Forms. Select all the verb forms that are a 2nd principal part.

_____ ambulāre

_____ bibō

_____ bibere

_____ dō

_____ dare

_____ venīre

_____ veniō

02-10 Complete the Story. Complete the following paragraph based on *Lectiō Secunda* with the appropriate words from the *Thēsaurus Verbōrum*. Be careful of singular and plural. Not every word in the word bank is used, and no word can be used twice.

Thēsaurus Verbōrum

ambulant	pecūniam	tabernam
cibum	respondent	venit
est	respondet	veniunt
iēiūnus	Rōmānus	

Sōl altus in caelō (1)_____. Vir ad tabernam (2)_____ et "Salvē," inquit,
"da mihi pānem et fīcōs." Valeria (3)_____ dat et Rōmānus (4)_____
dat. "Grātiās, domina," vir inquit, "Valē!"
"Valē," Valeria et Licinia (5)_____.

02-11 Derivatives in *Lectiō Secunda*. The following English words are derived from Latin words you saw in *Lectiō Secunda* in Chapter 2 of the textbook. The part in bold will help you recognize the Latin word. List the Latin word in the blank provided. Follow the model.

English Derivative	Latin Word
→ **a.m.** (ante **merīd**iem)	*merīdiēs*
1. **alt**imeter	_____
2. **ambul**atory	_____
3. **aqu**atic	_____
4. **vir**ility	_____
5. **popul**arity	_____
6. **mult**iply	_____

02-12 English Derivatives. Using your knowledge of the vocabulary of this chapter, match the word with its meaning.

1. altitude _____
2. virility _____
3. multiple _____
4. multitude _____
5. aqueous humor _____
6. ambulatory _____
7. perambulator (pram) _____

a. a large number of people
b. able to walk
c. baby carriage in Britain
d. height
e. many in number
f. masculinity
g. watery fluid in the eye

02-13 The Concept of Person: 2ⁿᵈ Person. All the verbs are marked in brackets in the following story. Select those that are in the 2ⁿᵈ person. If any are repeated, select them each time they appear.

George, Fred, and Martha [were walking] in the street one day when they [met] Julius Caesar.

"[Are] you who I [think] you [are]?" [asked] Martha.

"I [think] that you [know] who I [am]." Caesar replied.

George, who [knows] nothing of history, said, "I [am] a big fan. I [have seen] all your movies."

Fred [broke] in and [asked], "Could we [have] your autograph?"

Caesar said, "Of course you [can]," and quickly [wrote], "I [came], I [saw], I [conquered]."

"You [are] very kind," said Martha. "We [are] sorry to have bothered you."

02-14 The Concept of Person: 1ˢᵗ Person. All the verbs are marked in brackets in the following story. Select those that are in the 1ˢᵗ person. If any are repeated, select them each time they appear.

George, Fred, and Martha [were walking] in the street one day when they [met] Julius Caesar.

"Are you who I [think] you [are]?" asked Martha.

"I [think] that you [know] who I [am]." Caesar replied.

George, who [knows] nothing of history, said, "I [am] a big fan. I [have seen] all your movies."

Fred [broke] in and [asked], "Could we [have] your autograph?"

Caesar said, "Of course you [can]," and quickly [wrote], "I [came], I [saw], I [conquered]."

"You [are] very kind," said Martha. "We [are] sorry to have bothered you."

02-15 The Concept of Person: 3rd Person. All the verbs are marked in brackets in the following story. Select those that are in the 3rd person. If any are repeated, select them each time they appear.

George, Fred, and Martha [were walking] in the street one day when they [met] Julius Caesar.

"Are you who I think you [are]?" asked Martha.

"I [think] that you [know] who I [am]." Caesar replied.

George, who [knows] nothing of history, said, "I [am] a big fan. I [have seen] all your movies."

Fred [broke] in and [asked], "Could we [have] your autograph?"

Caesar said, "Of course you [can]," and quickly [wrote], "I [came], I [saw], I [conquered]."

"You [are] very kind," said Martha. "We [are] sorry to have bothered you."

02-16 The Concept of Person: Singular vs. Plural. Select the correct person (1st, 2nd, 3rd) and number (singular/plural) for the verb in bold. Follow the model.

→ ____c____ Valeria and Licinia **work** very hard in the snack shop.
  a. 1st singular   **b.** 2nd plural   **c.** 3rd plural   **d.** 1st plural

1. "Licinia, do you **know** where Flavia is?"
   a. 2nd plural   **b.** 1st singular   **c.** 2nd singular   **d.** 3rd singular

2. "No, but I **saw** her heading to the Forum."
   a. 2nd plural   **b.** 1st singular   **c.** 2nd singular   **d.** 3rd singular

3. Valeria and Licinia **leave** the snack shop to find Flavia.
   a. 3rd plural   **b.** 1st singular   **c.** 2nd singular   **d.** 3rd singular

4. "That silly girl," says Valeria. "We **have to** find her!"
   a. 2nd plural   **b.** 1st plural   **c.** 2nd singular   **d.** 3rd plural

5. "If they find her they will **think** she is a runaway."
   a. 3rd singular   **b.** 1st plural   **c.** 2nd singular   **d.** 3rd plural

6. "Wait! There she **is!**"
   a. 3rd singular   **b.** 2st plural   **c.** 2nd singular   **d.** 3rd plural

7. "Mistresses! I **am** so glad to see you. Don't be mad."
   a. 2nd plural   **b.** 1st singular   **c.** 2nd singular   **d.** 3rd singular

8. "See? Socrates **escaped** so I ran after him."
   a. 2nd plural   **b.** 1st singular   **c.** 2nd singular   **d.** 3rd singular

02-17 Saying Hello and Goodbye. Complete the following conversation with *Salvē, Salvēte, Valē,* or *Valēte* based on context and the number of people being addressed. Use the *Thēsaurus Verbōrum* for help with unfamiliar words.

Thēsaurus Verbōrum

ancilla maid servant   *domina* mistress   *domum* home, to home

Valeria et Flāvia in tabernā sunt. Licinia ad tabernam venit.

Valeria: "(1)_____, Licinia."

Licinia: " (2)_____, māter."

Flāvia ancilla: "(3)_____," inquit, "domina."

Vir ad tabernam venit et "(4) _____," inquit, "Valeria et Licinia."

Vir pecūniam dat et tunc ad Forum ambulat. Valeria "(5) _____," inquit.

Tunc Valeria domum ambulat et "Licinia et Flāvia," inquit, "(6) _____."

02-18 *Praenōmina Rōmāna.* Choose the correct abbreviation for each Roman *praenōmen*.

1. Aulus
   - **a.** A.
   - **b.** App.
   - **c.** Au.
2. Appius
   - **a.** A.
   - **b.** App.
   - **c.** Au.
3. Gāius
   - **a.** C.
   - **b.** G.
   - **c.** Ga.
4. Gnaeus
   - **a.** C.
   - **b.** Gn.
   - **c.** Cn.
5. Lūcius
   - **a.** L.
   - **b.** Lu.
   - **c.** Ls.
6. Marcus
   - **a.** M.
   - **b.** Ma.
   - **c.** Mc.
7. Publius
   - **a.** P.
   - **b.** Pu.
   - **c.** Pū.
8. Quintus
   - **a.** Q.
   - **b.** Qu.
   - **c.** Qt.
9. Sextus
   - **a.** S.
   - **b.** Se.
   - **c.** Sex.
10. Tiberius
   - **a.** T.
   - **b.** Ti(b).
   - **c.** Tb.

02-19 *Nōmina Rōmāna.* Is the word in bold a *praenōmen*, a *nōmen*, or a *cognōmen*? Select the correct answer for each.

1. Q. **Horātius** Flaccus
   - **a.** praenōmen
   - **b.** nōmen
   - **c.** cognōmen
2. P. Vergilius **Marō**
   - **a.** praenōmen
   - **b.** nōmen
   - **c.** cognōmen
3. T. **Līvius**
   - **a.** praenōmen
   - **b.** nōmen
   - **c.** cognōmen
4. **M.** Servīlius Sevērus
   - **a.** praenōmen
   - **b.** nōmen
   - **c.** cognōmen
5. M. **Tullius** Cicerō
   - **a.** praenōmen
   - **b.** nōmen
   - **c.** cognōmen

02-20 Complete the Sentence. Choose the word or phrase that best completes each sentence.

1. Alius venit et _____ poscit.
   a. sol   **b.** calidum   **c.** tibi

2. Da _____ calidum, sī placet.
   a. iēiūnus   **b.** mihi   **c.** in viīs

3. Dā mihi pānem et fīcōs, sī _____ placet.
   a. mihi   **b.** tibi   **c.** Valeria et Licinia

4. Diēs _____ est.
   a. iēiūnus   **b.** laetus   **c.** aestuōsus

5. In urbe multī Rōmānī in viīs _____.
   a. est   **b.** ambulat   **c.** sunt

6. _____ populī bibunt.
   a. iēiūnus   **b.** laetus   **c.** multī

7. Sōl altus in _____ est.
   a. tabernā   **b.** caelō   **c.** viīs

02-21 How Closely Did You Read? Read each description, then select the correct answer.

1. This refers to the individual spoken to:
   a. 1st person   **b.** 2nd person   **c.** 3rd person

2. The *Argīlētum* is:
   a. the street where Valeria's shop is located   **c.** the neighborhood in which Valeria lives
   b. another name for the Forum   **d.** a temple in the Forum

3. The family (*gens*) name of a Roman is the:
   a. *cognōmen*   **b.** *nōmen*   **c.** *praenōmen*

4. This means "sends greetings":
   a. S.D.   **b.** IMP.   **c.** S.V.V.

5. This refers to the individual speaking:
   a. 1st person   **b.** 2nd person   **c.** 3rd person

6. It's the third name of some Romans:
   a. *nōmen*   **b.** *cognōmen*   **c.** *praenōmen*

7. This refers to the individual spoken about:
   a. 1st person   **b.** 2nd person   **c.** 3rd person

8. It's the first name of a Roman:
   a. *cognōmen*   **b.** *nōmen*   **c.** *praenōmen*

9. This refers to the person saying "goodbye" to a group:
   a. salutatorian   **b.** *praenōmen*   **c.** valedictorian

10. If you are well, I am well:
    a. S.D.   **b.** S.V.V.   **c.** SAL.

02-22 Crossword Puzzle. Complete the puzzle with information from the chapter. A clue in quotes means that a definition in the other language is called for. Thus the clue "vir" is asking for the answer "man" and "man" is asking for "vir."

Across

3 – The street Valeria's shop is on
4 – A warm drink
8 – The abbreviation for this name is *C*
9 – "They are"
11 – Term that refers to the time of a verb's action
12 – Roman male's first name
15 – The abbreviation for this name is *P*
16 – "Snack shop"
17 – The one spoken to
20 – Gives the opening address at a graduation
23 – "Ad"
25 – "Goodbye" (to one)
26 – "Hello!" (to many)
27 – A Roman's family name

Down

1 – "Goodbye" (to many)
2 – "Male student"
5 – "Female student"
6 – "Teacher, female"
7 – The one speaking
10 – Gives the farewell address at a graduation
11 – The one spoken about
13 – "Teacher, male"
14 – "Hello!" (to one)
18 – Last part of a Roman's name
19 – "Bibit"
21 – "Water"
22 – "I walk"
24 – "They walk"

3 Negōtium Bonum

03-01 Complete the Story. The following sentences make up a small, connected narrative based on *Lectiō Prīma*. Complete each sentence by selecting a word from the *Thēsaurus Verbōrum*. Not every word and phrase is used, but none is used twice.

Thēsaurus Verbōrum

bonum	labōrat	ūnum virum
bonus	laeta	venit
cibum et pōtum	laetae	veniunt
edit	pecūnia	vir
edunt	pecūniam	virī
labōrant	salvē	
	salvēte	

1. Multī virī ad tabernam _____.
2. Vir "_____," inquit, "domina."
3. Valeria _____ dat.
4. _____ "Grātiās," inquit, "domina."
5. Aliī virī sōlum bibunt et _____.
6. Virī _____ dant.
7. Tunc _____ ad Forum adveniunt.
8. Valeria et Licinia et Flāvia strēnuē _____.
9. Valeria _____ est.
10. Hodiē negōtium _____ est.

03-02 Finding Subjects in English. Select the subject in each sentence. If there is more than one subject in the sentence, select them all. Select only the noun or pronoun, not the articles (a, the). All these words would be in the nominative case in Latin.

1. Valeria gives food to the men.
2. While Valeria works, the men eat and drink.
3. Flavia works hard too, but she does not earn a salary.
4. The men pay good money for the food Valeria prepares, and they are glad to do so.
5. Valeria's shop is near the Forum so that she can attract many potential customers.
6. The monkey also helps bring in customers, and he seems to enjoy it.

03-03 Finding Direct Objects in English.

Select every direct object in each sentence. If there is more than one direct object in the sentence, select them all. Select only the noun or pronoun, not the articles (a, the). All of these words would be in the accusative case in Latin.

1. Valeria gives food to the men.
2. While Valeria works, the men eat their food and drink their wine.
3. Flavia works hard too, but she does not earn a salary.
4. The men pay good money for the food Valeria prepares, and they are glad to do so.
5. Valeria's shop is near the Forum so that she can attract many potential customers.
6. The monkey also helps bring in customers, and he seems to enjoy his job.

03-04 Word Substitution: Nominative Case.

Substitute each word in parentheses for the word in bold in the pattern sentence. Adjust the number (singular, plural) as necessary to keep it the same as the original. Follow the model.

→ **Virī** pecūniam dant. (fēmina, ancilla, Rōmānus)

 Fēminae pecūniam dant.

 Ancillae pecūniam dant.

 Rōmānī pecūniam dant.

Valeria cibum et pōtum dat. (ancilla, vir, fēmina)

1. _____ cibum et pōtum dat.
2. _____ cibum et pōtum dat.
3. _____ cibum et pōtum dat.

Valeria et Licinia virōs vident. (fēmina, ancilla, Flāvia et Licinia)

4. _____ virōs vident.
5. _____ virōs vident.
6. _____ virōs vident.

Valeria laeta est. (fēmina, ancilla, Licinia)

7. _____ laeta est.
8. _____ laeta est.
9. _____ laeta est.

Vir ad tabernam venit. (ancilla, Rōmānus, Valeria)

10. _____ ad tabernam venit.
11. _____ ad tabernam venit.
12. _____ ad tabernam venit.

Ancillae strēnuē in tabernā labōrant. (fēmina, vir, Rōmānus)

13. _____ strēnuē in tabernā labōrant.
14. _____ strēnuē in tabernā labōrant.
15. _____ strēnuē in tabernā labōrant.

03-05 Word Substitution: Accusative Case. Substitute each word in parentheses for the word in bold in the pattern sentence. Put it in the accusative case and keep the number the same as the original. Follow the model.

→ Vir **fēminam** videt. (taberna, ancilla, vir)

    Vir *tabernam* videt.

    Vir *ancillam* videt.

    Vir *virum* videt.

Valeria **ancillam** videt. (pecūnia, ficus, cibus)

1. Valeria _____ videt.

2. Valeria _____ videt.

3. Valeria _____ videt.

Fēminae **ficōs** vident. (Rōmānus, vir, ancilla)

4. Fēminae _____ vident.

5. Fēminae _____ vident.

6. Fēminae _____ vident.

Rōmānī **cibum** vident. (filia, vir, fēmina)

7. Rōmānī _____ vident.

8. Rōmānī _____ vident.

9. Rōmānī _____ vident.

Fīliae **Rōmānōs** vident. (fēmina, vir, ancilla)

10. Fīliae _____ vident.

11. Fīliae _____ vident.

12. Fīliae _____ vident.

03-06 Finding Nominative Case Nouns and Adjectives. Select every noun or adjective that is in the nominative case. If a word is repeated, select every instance of it.

Virī pecūniam dant et tunc abeunt (*go away*).

Subitō, multī virī simul adveniunt et fēminās vident. Valeria multōs virōs videt et "Salvēte!" inquit.

Cibum et pōtum poscunt. Valeria et Licinia et Flāvia strēnuē labōrant sed domina laeta est, quod multī virī multam pecūniam significant.

03-07 Finding Accusative Case Nouns and Adjectives. Select every noun or adjective that is in the accusative case. If a word is repeated, select every instance of it.

Virī pecūniam dant et tunc abeunt (*go away*).

Subitō, multī virī simul adveniunt et fēminās vident. Valeria multōs virōs videt et "Salvēte!" inquit.

Cibum et pōtum poscunt. Valeria et Licinia et Flāvia strēnuē labōrant sed domina laeta est, quod multī virī multam pecūniam significant.

03-08 Derivatives in *Lectiōnēs Prīma et Secunda*. The following is a list of Latin words you saw in the two *lectiōnēs* in Chapter 3. For each one, give at least one English derivative. Follow the model.

→ pictūra   *picture, pictorial*

1. secunda   _____

2. taberna   _____

3. significant   _____

4. respondent   _____

5. nihil   _____

6. negōtium   _____

7. vīnō   _____

03-09 Translation Practice. Practice your grasp of endings by selecting the proper translation for the Latin sentence. Let the endings, rather than your sense of English word order, be your guide.

1. *Vir bonus est.*
- **a.** You are a good man.
- **b.** The man is good.
- **c.** The men are good.

2. *Fēminae laetae nōn sunt.*
- **a.** The woman is not happy.
- **b.** The happy women are here.
- **c.** The women are not happy.

3. *Virum fēminae vident.*
- **a.** The man sees the woman.
- **b.** The woman sees the man.
- **c.** The women see the man.
- **d.** The women see the men.

4. *Fēminās laetās vir nōn videt.*
- **a.** The happy women don't see the man.
- **b.** The man doesn't see the happy women.
- **c.** The happy woman doesn't see the man.
- **d.** The men don't see the happy woman.

5. *Pecūnia multōs virōs habet.*
- **a.** Many men have money.
- **b.** The men have much money.
- **c.** The man has a lot of money.
- **d.** Money possesses many men.

6. *Virī laetī multam pecūniam habent.*
- **a.** Many happy men have money.
- **b.** The happy man has a lot of money.
- **c.** Money possesses many happy men.
- **d.** Happy men have lots of money.

03-10 Identifying Declensions. For each sentence, identify the declension of the word in bold. Follow the model.

→ In tabernā **Valeria** pōtum vendit.
- **a.** *1ˢᵗ declension*
- **b.** 2ⁿᵈ declension

1. In tabernā Valeria **pōtum** vendit.
- **a.** 1ˢᵗ declension
- **b.** 2ⁿᵈ declension

2. Tertius **Rōmānus** advenit, et valdē iēiūnus est.
- **a.** 1ˢᵗ declension
- **b.** 2ⁿᵈ declension

3. Valeria multam **pecūniam** habet.
- **a.** 1ˢᵗ declension
- **b.** 2ⁿᵈ declension

4. Valeria multās **fēminās** in tabernā videt.
- **a.** 1ˢᵗ declension
- **b.** 2ⁿᵈ declension

5. Multī **virī** multam pecūniam significant.
- **a.** 1ˢᵗ declension
- **b.** 2ⁿᵈ declension

03-11 Case Identification: Nominative. Select each word marked in brackets in the following paragraph that is in the nominative case. Include adjectives and nouns.

In tabernā [Valeria] [pōtum] et [cibum] vendit. [Rōmānus] venit et valdē [ieiūnus] est.
Valeria [multōs virōs] in tabernā videt. [Multī virī] [multam pecūniam] significant et Valeria [laeta] est.

03-12 Case Identification: Accusative. Select each word marked in brackets in the following paragraph that is in the accusative case. Include adjectives and nouns.

In tabernā [Valeria pōtum] et [cibum] vendit. [Rōmānus] venit et valdē [ieiūnus] est.
Valeria [multōs virōs] in tabernā videt. [Multī virī] [multam pecūniam] significant et Valeria [laeta] est.

03-13 Word Identification: Number. Select all of the plural nouns and adjectives in the following paragraph, regardless of their case or declension.

In tabernā Valeria pōtum et cibum vendit. Rōmānus venit et valdē ieiūnus est.
Valeria multōs virōs in tabernā videt. Multī virī multam pecūniam significant et Valeria laeta est.

03-14 Declension Identification: 1ˢᵗ Declension. Select all of the 1ˢᵗ declension nouns and adjectives, regardless of their case.

Ancilla Flāvia strēnuē labōrat et nōn laeta est. Multī Rōmānī veniunt et cibum poscunt. Valeria Flāviam videt et clāmat, "Mē adiuvāte! Dā mihi aquam et vīnum!" Virī pecūniam dant et ad Forum ambulant.

03-15 Reading Comprehension in *Lectiō Secunda*. Select the order that puts the sentences in the same order in which they occur in *Lectiō Secunda*.

a. Valeria nōn laeta est, sed nihil dīcit.
b. Nunc virī pecūniam dant et ad Forum ambulant.
c. Flāvia ficōs capit.
d. Valeria clāmat: "Mē adiuvāte!"
e. Quīnque ficī ad terram cadunt.

1. c, e, b, a, d
2. d, c, e, a, b
3. b, a, c, e, d
4. e, a, c, d, b
5. c, d, e, a, b

03-16 *Verba Discenda* Chapters 2–3. Match the Latin word with its English meaning. All the Latin words are from the *Verba Discenda* in Chapters 2 and 3.

1. altus _____
2. ambulō_____
3. aqua _____
4. dant _____
5. fēmina _____
6. laetus _____
7. multus _____
8. pecūnia _____
9. salvē_____

a. but
b. happy
c. hello
d. high
e. walk
f. money
g. much
h. only
i. shop

10. sed ____   j. are

11. sōlum ____   k. give

12. sunt ____   l. water

13. taberna ____   m. wine

14. vīnum ____   n. woman

03-17 Subjects, Objects, and Verbs. Select the correct grammatical function for the bold words in each sentence.

1. Hodie **negōtium** bonum est.

   a. subject   b. object   c. verb

2. Fīlia **pecūniam** poscit.

   a. subject   b. object   c. verb

3. **Fēminae laetae** "Valēte!" clāmant.

   a. subject   b. object   c. verb

4. Multī virī ad tabernam **veniunt.**

   a. subject   b. object   c. verb

5. **Flāvia et Licinia** strēnuē labōrant.

   a. subject   b. object   c. verb

6. Ūnus Rōmānus **vīnum** bibit.

   a. subject   b. object   c. verb

7. Fēminae **multōs virōs** vident.

   a. subject   b. object   c. verb

8. **Fēminae** multōs virōs vident.

   a. subject   b. object   c. verb

03-18 Plural to Singular: 1st and 2nd Declensions. Change the words in bold to their singular forms, keeping the same case (nominative or accusative) as the original word. Follow the model.

→ **Magistrī** ad Forum veniunt. _____*Magister*_____

1. **Fēminae** ad tabernam ambulant. _____

2. Ancilla quinque **virōs** videt. _____

3. **Fīcī** ad terram cadunt. _____

4. **Ancillae** strēnuē labōrant. _____

5. Valeria quinque **fēminās** videt. _____

6. **Virī** multam pecūniam dant. _____

03-19 Case and Number Analysis. Select the case and number that correctly identifies each Latin word. Follow the model.

	Case	**Number**
→ fīcōs	nominative / <u>accusative</u>	singular / <u>plural</u>
1. *ancillae*	nominative / accusative	singular / plural
2. *Rōmānus*	nominative / accusative	singular / plural
3. *vir*	nominative / accusative	singular / plural
4. *pecūniam*	nominative / accusative	singular / plural
5. *virī*	nominative / accusative	singular / plural
6. *Rōmanōs*	nominative / accusative	singular / plural
7. *virum*	nominative / accusative	singular / plural
8. *fēminās*	nominative / accusative	singular / plural

03-20 How Closely Did You Read? Complete each sentence with the correct word from the *Thēsaurus Verbōrum*.

Thēsaurus Verbōrum

accusative	declension	subject
basilica	nominative	*taberna*
calidum	predicate nominative	transitive
Cūria Iūlia	*rostra*	

1. The full and proper name for the Senate House is _____.

2. A _____ is a snack shop.

3. The term _____ refers to the one who performs the action of an active verb.

4. The direct object of a transitive verb goes in the _____ case.

5. _____ was a spiced hot wine drink popular in ancient Rome.

6. The _____ is the speaker's platform in the Forum.

7. The subject of a verb is in the _____ case.

8. The grammatical term _____ refers to verbs which can take direct objects.

9. The term _____ refers to a group of nouns that have the same endings.

10. Intransitive verbs often link a noun and a _____.

11. Latin word for a law court is a _____.

03-21 Crossword Puzzle. Complete the puzzle with information from the chapter.

Across

2 – Full name of the Roman Senate House
4 – This kind of verb can take a predicate nominative
7 – "Nothing"
8 – "Solum"
11 – Another name for a *taberna*
15 – "Then"
17 – The direct object uses this case
19 – "Semper"
20 – Latin word for something served at the *taberna*
21 – "Answer, reply"

Down

1 – "Hi, y'all!"
3 – A hot drink favored by the Romans
5 – "Now"
6 – A verb that takes a direct object
9 – The subject goes in this case
10 – Latin nouns are grouped into five of these
12 – "Money"
13 – Latin is an _____ language
14 – Speakers' platform in the Forum
16 – "Quod"
18 – Third principal part of *capiō*

4 Intrat Hermēs

04-01 Complete the Story: *Lēctiō Prīma.* The following sentences make up a short narrative based on *Lēctiō Prīma.* Complete each sentence by filling in the blank with a word from the *Thēsaurus Verbōrum.* Every word is used, and none is used twice.

Thēsaurus Verbōrum

ambulat	lūdum
domum	magistrī
fēminae	parātus
heri	salūtat
Lūciī	tabernam

1. Postrīdiē _____ iterum in Valeriae tabernā sunt.
2. Hodiē, sīcut _____, aestuōsus est.
3. Hermēs ad Valeriae _____ venit.
4. Hermēs paedagōgus _____ est.
5. Cōtīdiē māne Lūcius ad lūdum magistrī _____.
6. Nōmen _____ Chīrōn est.
7. Cōtīdiē māne Hermēs Lūcium ad _____ magistrī dūcit.
8. Sērius Hermēs Lūcium _____ rursus dūcit.
9. Nunc Hermēs dūcere Lūcium domum _____ est.
10. Venit ad Valeriae tabernam et eam _____.

04-02 Recognizing Genitives. Select all the genitives, singular and plural, from the following list.

_____ aqua	_____ discipulum
_____ aquae	_____ fēminae
_____ aquam	_____ fēminam
_____ aquās	_____ fēminārum
_____ cibī	_____ magister
_____ cibōrum	_____ magistra
_____ cibum	_____ magistrārum
_____ discipulae	_____ magistrae
_____ discipulam	_____ magistrum
_____ discipulārum	_____ virī
_____ discipulī	_____ virōs

04-03 Forming Genitives. Form the genitive (singular or plural, as asked) of the following nouns. Then translate that form two different ways (using 's/s' or "of"). Follow the model.

➡ **discipula (pl.)**   **discipulārum**   **of the students, the students'**

1. discipulus (sing.)   a. _____   b. _____
2. ancilla (sing.)   a. _____   b. _____
3. cibus (pl.)   a. _____   b. _____
4. fēmina (sing.)   a. _____   b. _____
5. vir (pl.)   a. _____   b. _____
6. magister (pl.)   a. _____   b. _____

04-04 Identifying Case Endings. Select the word that is in the case indicated.

1. genitive singular:
   a. aquam   **b.** aquās   **c.** aqua   **d.** aquae

2. accusative singular:
   a. pecūnia   **b.** pecūniae   **c.** pecūniam   **d.** pecūniās

3. accusative plural:
   a. vir   **b.** virī   **c.** virōs   **d.** virum

4. genitive plural:
   a. discipulī   **b.** discipulōrum   **c.** discipulus   **d.** discipulōs

5. nominative singular:
   a. discipula   **b.** discipulam   **c.** discipulārum   **d.** discipulās

6. accusative singular:
   a. cibum   **b.** cibōs   **c.** cibus   **d.** cibī

7. nominative plural:
   a. fēminārum   **b.** fēminae   **c.** fēminam   **d.** fēminās

8. accusative plural:
   a. magister   **b.** magistrī   **c.** magistrum   **d.** magistrōs

9. genitive singular:
   a. magistrae   **b.** magistra   **c.** magistrās   **d.** magistrārum

10. nominative singular:
    a. tabernārum   **b.** taberna   **c.** tabernam   **d.** tabernās

04-05 Reviewing the Genitive.
Change the number of the genitive in the following phrases, i.e., if the genitive is singular, make it plural and if it is plural, make it singular.

1. virī _____

2. familiae _____

3. filiōrum _____

4. magistrī _____

5. populī _____

6. filiārum _____

04-06 Latin Personal Endings and Pronouns.
Select the English pronoun you would use to translate a verb with the given personal ending.

1. -s _____   **a.** I

2. -t _____   **b.** you (sing.)

3. -mus _____   **c.** he, she, it

4. -tis _____   **d.** we

5. -ō _____   **e.** you (all)

6. -nt _____   **f.** they

04-07 Personal Endings: English to Latin.
Select the Latin word that best translates the English verb form.

1. you drink:
   a. *bibō*   **b.** *bibit*   **c.** *bibis*   **d.** *bibimus*

2. I put:
   a. *pōnō*   **b.** *pōnimus*   **c.** *pōnis*   **d.** *pōnunt*

3. we lead:
   a. *dūcimus*   **b.** *dūcō*   **c.** *dūcit*   **d.** *dūcunt*

4. they act:
   a. *agit*   **b.** *agunt*   **c.** *agō*   **d.** *agitis*

5. you greet:
   a. *salūtō*   **b.** *salūtat*   **c.** *salūtātis*   **d.** *salūtant*

6. she drinks:
   a. *bibō*   **b.** *bibit*   **c.** *bibis*   **d.** *bibimus*

7. we put:
   a. *pōnō*   **b.** *pōnimus*   **c.** *pōnis*   **d.** *pōnunt*

8. they lead:
   a. *dūcimus*   **b.** *dūcō*   **c.** *dūcit*   **d.** *dūcunt*

9. you act:
   a. *agit*   **b.** *agunt*   **c.** *agō*   **d.** *agitis*

10. he takes:
    a. *capitis*   **b.** *capiō*   **c.** *capit*   **d.** *capiunt*

04-08 Personal Endings: Latin to English. Choose the best translation for each Latin verb. Pay careful attention to the personal endings.

1. *ambulāmus:*
- **a.** they walk
- **b.** we walk
- **c.** I walk

2. *respondēs:*
- **a.** he responds
- **b.** I respond
- **c.** you respond

3. *vendit:*
- **a.** I sell
- **b.** she sells
- **c.** we sell

4. *veniunt:*
- **a.** they come
- **b.** we come
- **c.** I come

5. *sumus:*
- **a.** they are
- **b.** we are
- **c.** I am

6. *ambulātis:*
- **a.** they walk
- **b.** we walk
- **c.** you walk

7. *respondēmus:*
- **a.** he responds
- **b.** I respond
- **c.** we respond

8. *vendis:*
- **a.** you sell
- **b.** she sells
- **c.** we sell

9. *veniō:*
- **a.** they come
- **b.** we come
- **c.** I come

10. *dat:*
- **a.** he gives
- **b.** we give
- **c.** I give

04-09 Subject-Verb Agreement. Complete the verb form in the target sentence to match each set of subjects. Use the *Thēsaurus Verbōrum* for unfamiliar words. Follow the model.

Thēsaurus Verbōrum

ego I   *tū* you (sing.)   *nōs* we   *vōs* you (pl.)

→ Valeria et Flāvia labōrant.

Ego labōr_____	Ego labōrō.
Tū labōr_____	Tū labōrās.
Tū et ego labōr_____	Tū et ego labōrāmus.
Tū et Maria labōr_____	Tū et Maria labōrātis.
Maria et Marcus labōr_____	Maria et Marcus labōrant.

Flāvia in viā ambulat.

1. Flāvia et Valeria in viā ambul_____

2. Flāvia et tū in viā ambul_____

3. Tū in viā ambul_____

4. Vōs et ego in viā ambul_____

5. Nōs in viā ambul_____

Multī virī fēminās in tabernā vident.

6. Nōs Valeriam in tabernā vid_____

7. Nōs et tū Valeriam in tabernā vid_____

8. Multae fēminae Valeriam in tabernā vid_____

9. Tū et ancilla Valeriam in tabernā vid_____

10. Marcus et tū Valeriam in tabernā vid_____

04-10 English Derivatives. Select the word that correctly completes each sentence.

1. I have a (**capitol/capital**) idea!
2. Let's go to the nation's (**capitol/capital**).
3. We will visit (**Capitol/Capital**) Hill.
4. From here we can see all the Greek (**capitols/capitals**) on the Treasury Building!
5. Your reports on the trip are due Tuesday. Be careful of your use of (**capitol/capital**) letters.

04-11 Comprehension. Use the *Thēsaurus Verbōrum* to fill in the blanks in this narrative based on *Lectiō Prīma*. No word is used more than once.

Thēsaurus Verbōrum

Caeciliae	familiā	tabernam
Chīrōn	labōrant	Valeriae
discipulī	lūdum	venit
discipulum	paedagōgus	veniunt
fēminae	salūtat	

Postrīdiē trēs (1)_____ iterum in tabernā sunt. (2)_____ taberna est.
Valeria, Licinia et Flāvia in tabernā (3)_____. Hodiē, sīcut herī, aestuōsus est. Multī
populī in Forō ambulant et ad Valeriae (4)_____ veniunt. Hermēs ad Valeriae tabernam
(5)_____. Hermēs Lūciī (6)_____ est. Lūcius fīlius Servīliī et
(7)_____ est. In Servīliī (8)_____ duo fīliī sunt, Marcus et Lūcius.
Cōtīdiē māne Lūcius et paedagōgus ad lūdum magistrī (9)_____. Nōmen magistrī est
(10)_____. In lūdō multī (11)_____ sunt. Cōtīdiē māne Lūcius ad
(12)_____ magistrī venit. Paedagōgus (13)_____ ad lūdum magistrī
dūcit. Nunc Hermēs dūcere Lūcium domum parātus est. Paedagōgus ad Valeriae tabernam venit et fēmina
paedagōgum (14)_____.

04-12 Translating *et* vs. *et...et*. Translate each sentence to show that you understand the proper uses of *et* (and) and *et...et* (both ...and). Follow the model.

→ Valeria cibum et pōtum dat.   *Valeria gives food and drink.*
  Valeria et cibum et pōtum dat.   *Valeria gives both food and drink.*

1. Virī et fēminae ad tabernam veniunt. _____
2. Et virī et fēminae ad tabernam veniunt. _____
3. Valeria et ancilla pōtum dant. _____
4. Et Valeria et ancilla pōtum dant. _____
5. Fēminae et virī et cibum et pōtum poscunt. _____
6. Fēminae et ancillae in Forō ambulant. _____
7. Et fēminae et ancillae ad Forum ambulant. _____
8. Fēminae et ad Forum et ad tabernam ambulant. _____

04-13 Translating *aut* vs. *aut...aut*. Translate these sentences to show that you understand the use of *aut* and *aut...aut*. Follow the model.

→ Da mihi pānem aut fīcōs.   *Give me bread or figs.*
   Da mihi aut pānem aut fīcōs.   *Give me either bread or figs.*

1. Valeria aut Flāvia in tabernā est. _____

2. Aut Valeria aut Flāvia in tabernā labōrat. _____

3. Aut Marcus aut Lūcius Servīliī fīlius est. _____

4. Fēminae aut ad Forum aut ad tabernam ambulant. _____

04-14 Reading Comprehension. Number the following sentences according to the order in which they actually occur in *Lectiō Secunda*. Put 1 next to the sentence that should come first, 2 next to the one that should come second, and so forth.

1. Valeria vīnum aquamque in pōculō pōnit. _____

2. Hermēs sitiens est et pōtum poscit. _____

3. Hermēs vīnumque aquamque bibit et laetus est. _____

4. Ad Valeriae tabernam Hermēs ambulat. _____

5. Hermēs pecūniam dat et saccum in mensā pōnit. _____

6. Paedagōgus Valeriam videt salūtatque. _____

04-15 How Closely Did You Read? Fill in the blank with the word, name, phrase, or ending from the *Thēsaurus Verbōrum* that best fits the description. Not every entry is used.

Thēsaurus Verbōrum

accusative	*mulsum*	Petronius
Bonum!	*-mus*	Pliny the Elder
Capitōlium	*-ne*	*Quid agis?*
Cato the Elder	nominative	Rostra
Est! Est!! Est!!!	*-nt*	*-tis*
genitive	Palatine	*Vale!*

1. _____ is attached to the end of a word in Latin to indicate that a question is being asked.

2. The _____ is a case used in Latin to show possession.

3. _____ is a wine drink heavily flavored with honey, very popular with the lower-classes in Rome.

4. _____ is a Latin personal ending which means "we."

5. _____ means "How are you?" in Latin.

6. _____ is a Roman writer who said that "In wine is truth."

7. _____ was the first Roman to write about wine cultivation.

8. _____ is the Roman hill that gives its name to many modern terms about government in the United States.

9. _____ is the Latin name for a modern wine.

10. _____ is the Roman hill where the imperial palaces were built.

04-16 Verba Discenda. Match the Latin Word with its English equivalent.

1. *agō, agere, ēgī, actum* _____
2. *aut ...aut* _____
3. *bene* _____
4. *cupiō, cupere, cupīvī/cupiī, cupītum* _____
5. *domus, -ī* f. _____
6. *dūcō, dūcere, dūxī, ductum* _____
7. *et ...et* _____
8. *fīlius, -ī* m. _____
9. *hodiē* _____
10. *iterum* _____
11. *lūdus, -ī* m. _____
12. *māne* _____
13. *pōnō, pōnere, posuī, positum* _____
14. *populus, -ī* m. _____
15. *-que* _____
16. *salūtō, salūtāre, salūtāvī, salūtātum* _____

a. act, do, lead, drive
b. again
c. and
d. both ...and
e. early in the morning
f. either ...or
g. greet
h. home, house
i. lead
j. people
k. put, place
l. school, game
m. son
n. today
o. well
p. wish, want to

04-17 *Verba Discenda:* Derivatives. Using your knowledge of the *Verba Discenda* for this chapter, select the best definition for the words and phrases given.

1. concupiscence _____
2. ductile _____
3. iteration _____
4. ludicrous _____
5. populous _____
6. posit _____
7. reagent _____
8. reductio ad absurdum _____
9. beneficiary _____
10. transpose _____

a. someone who profits from a life insurance policy
b. laughable
c. crowded with people
d. abnormally strong desire
e. able to be drawn out into wire; easily led or influenced
f. action of repeating something
g. a chemical that reacts to another
h. the leading of something to a ridiculous conclusion
i. to lay down the premise for something
j. to put in a different place or order

Across

3 – Added to the end of a word to indicate a sentence is a yes/no question

5 – The president of Italy lives on this hill

7 – Slave in charge of a young boy

8 – "To home"

9 – The road on which victorious generals celebrated their triumphs

11 – First Roman to write about wine

12 – "either … or"

13 – "both … and"

17 – A wine from Montefiascone

18 – A short word stuck on the end of a longer word

21 – *Vīnum incendit* _____

22 – The case used by the subject of a sentence

Down

1 – Its volcanic soil produced fine grapes and wine

2 – The case that shows possession

4 – "Field of Mars"

6 – "To wish"

9 – *In* _____ *vēritās est*

10 – The case used by the direct object of a verb

14 – Rome's river

15 – "the women's"

16 – "of the woman"

19 – *Magister in Lūcii lūdō*

20 – The decorated top of a column

5 In Forō

05-01 Interrogatives: -ne, num, or nonne? Read each English interrogative sentence carefully, then select the word that would start the sentence in Latin.

1. John: Do you want to go bowling tonight?
    a. *-ne*   **b.** *num*   **c.** *nōnne*

2. Mary: You don't expect me actually to go bowling, do you?
    a. *-ne*   **b.** *num*   **c.** *nōnne*

3. John: But you like bowling, don't you?
    a. *-ne*   **b.** *num*   **c.** *nōnne*

4. Mary: You don't have a clue, do you?
    a. *-ne*   **b.** *num*   **c.** *nōnne*

5. John: OK. Let me try again. Do you want to go to the monster truck rally?
    a. *-ne*   **b.** *num*   **c.** *nōnne*

6. Mary: You actually think I'd go there, don't you?
    a. *-ne*   **b.** *num*   **c.** *nōnne*

05-02 Questions in Latin. Select the best translation for each Latin question. Don't be led astray by the facts of the story. Translate each question on its own.

1. *Nōnne Hermēs sīmiam in tabernā videt?*
    a. Hermes doesn't see a monkey in the snack shop, does he?
    b. Does Hermes see a monkey in the snack shop?
    c. Hermes sees a monkey in the snack shop, doesn't he?

2. *Estne sīmiae nōmen Sōcratēs?*
    a. The monkey's name is Socrates, isn't it?
    b. The monkey's name isn't Socrates, is it?
    c. Is the monkey's name Socrates?

3. *Num Valeria Liciniae māter est?*
    a. Is Valeria Licinia's mother?
    b. Valeria is Licinia's mother, isn't she?
    c. Valeria isn't Licinia's mother, is she?

4. *Nōnne Rōmānī calidum bibunt?*
    a. Romans drink *calidum*, don't they?
    b. Do Romans drink *calidum*?
    c. Romans don't drink *calidum*, do they?

5. *Estne negōtium bonum hodiē?*
    a. Business is good today, isn't it?
    b. Business isn't good today, is it?
    c. Is business good today?

6. *Num Valeria Flāviae māter est?*
    a. Valeria is Flavia's mother, isn't she?
    b. Valeria isn't Flavia's mother, is she?
    c. Is Valeria Flavia's mother?

05-03 Translating Questions in Latin.
Translate each of the following questions into English in a way that shows you understand the force of *num* or *nōnne*. The questions are based on *Lectiō Prīma*. Follow the model.

→ Nōnne Hermēs sīmiam in tabernā videt?
   Hermes sees the monkey at the snack shop, doesn't he?

1. Num Hermēs sīmiam in tabernā videt? _____

2. Nōnne nōmen sīmia habet? _____

3. Num Hermēs rīdet? _____

4. Num Sōcratēs vīnum cupit? _____

5. Nōnne Sōcratēs vīnum cupit? _____

6. Nōnne sīmiae iocōs amant? _____

05-04 Prepositions.
Translate the following sentences into English.

1. Sōcratēs per viam currit. _____

2. Sōcratēs in tabernā est. _____

3. Sōcratēs ē viā currit. _____

4. Sōcratēs inter viam et Forum stat. _____

5. Sōcratēs ad paedagōgum currit. _____

6. Sōcratēs post templum stat. _____

7. Sōcratēs in Basilicam currit. _____

8. Paedagōgus ā tabernā currit. _____

05-05 Reading Comprehension: *Lectiō Prīma.*
Number the following sentences to put them in order, based on *Lectiō Prīma*.

Subitō Hermēs ad sīmiam salit, sed eum nōn capit. _____

"Ecce!" Hermēs clāmat, "Sīmia saccum meum habet!" _____

Hermēs rīdet. "Salvē, sīmia!" paedagōgus inquit. _____

Hermēs sīmiam in tabernā videt. _____

Hermēs "Cupisne," inquit, "vīnum, Sōcratēs?" _____

Sīmia subitō saccum paedagōgī rapit. _____

05-06 Dictionary Entries: Verbs. Select the completion for each statement or response to the question based on the following verbs:

salūtō, salūtāre, salūtāvī, salūtātum

respondeō, respondēre, respondī, responsum

1. *Salūtāre* is best translated:
   a. I greet   **b.** I have greeted   **c.** having been greeted   **d.** to greet

2. *Salūtāvī* is best translated:
   a. I greet   **b.** I have greeted   **c.** having been greeted   **d.** to greet

3. *Salūtātum* is best translated
   a. I greet   **b.** I have greeted   **c.** having been greeted   **d.** to greet

4. *Salūtāre* tells you that this verb is in what conjugation?
   a. first   **b.** second   **c.** third   **d.** fourth

5. The principal part that translates "I have responded" is
   a. *respondeō*   **b.** *respondēre*   **c.** *respondī*   **d.** *responsum*

6. *Respondēre* tells you that this verb is in what conjugation?
   a. first   **b.** second   **c.** third   **d.** fourth

05-07 1ˢᵗ and 2ⁿᵈ Conjugation Dictionary Entries. Use these four verbs to complete the following statements:

clāmō (1)

habeō, habēre, habuī, habitum

stō, stāre, stetī, statum

videō, vidēre, vīdī, vīsum

1. *Clāmātum* means
   a. I have called   **b.** to call   **c.** having been called   **d.** I call

2. *Vīdī* means
   a. I have seen   **b.** to see   **c.** having been seen   **d.** I see

3. "I stood" in Latin is
   a. *stō*   **b.** *stāre*   **c.** *stetī*   **d.** *statum*

4. *Vīsum* means
   a. I have seen   **b.** to see   **c.** having been seen   **d.** I see

5. "To have" in Latin is
   a. *habeō*   **b.** *habēre*   **c.** *habuī*   **d.** *habitum*

6. Which one is not 2ⁿᵈ conjugation?
   a. clāmāre   **b.** *vidēre*   **c.** *habēre*   **d.** *monēre*

05-08 *Animālia Rōmāna.* Find the animal hidden in each "-ine" word. If you don't recognize the animal, look the word up in an English dictionary.

1. canine ____	**a.** bear
2. feline ____	**b.** bull
3. equine ____	**c.** cat
4. piscine ____	**d.** cow
5. porcine ____	**e.** crow
6. bovine ____	**f.** deer
7. aquiline ____	**g.** dog
8. ovine ____	**h.** donkey
9. ursine ____	**i.** dove
10. serpentine ____	**j.** eagle
11. asinine ____	**k.** fish
12. lupine ____	**l.** fox
13. vulpine ____	**m.** goose
14. corvine ____	**n.** horse
15. leonine ____	**o.** lion
16. anserine ____	**p.** pig
17. cervine ____	**q.** seal
18. phocine ____	**r.** sheep
19. columbine ____	**s.** snake
20. taurine ____	**t.** wolf

05-09 How Closely Did You Read? Select the correct answer from the *Thēsaurus Verbōrum* to answer each of the following questions.

Thēsaurus Verbōrum

Templum Castorum	Mausoleum of Halicarnassus
Templum Dīvī Iūliī	*-ne*
Templum Vestae	*nōnne*
conjugation	*num*
Mausōlēum Augustī	preposition

1. Which Wonder of the Ancient World did Augustus imitate in building his tomb in Rome? ____
2. Which word did Romans use to introduce a question expecting a "yes" answer? ____
3. Which temple in the Roman Forum was dedicated to twin gods? ____
4. Which syllable did Romans add to a word to indicate that a simple yes/no question was being asked? ____
5. Which term is used to describe groups of Latin verbs that act alike? ____
6. Which building in Rome contained cinerary urns of Augustus and his family? ____
7. Which word did Romans use to introduce a question expecting a "no" answer? ____
8. Which part of speech is used with nouns and pronouns to express direction, the source of an action, or relationship? ____
9. At which temple in the Roman Forum did a fire always burn? ____
10. At which temple in the Roman Forum did Hermes get his wallet back? ____

Name: _____   Date: _____

05-10 Why Learn *Verba Discenda*? The *Verba Discenda* in each chapter are determined by frequency; i.e., the more likely you are to see these words, the more important they are. Translate the following sentences into English. They consist **only** of *Verba Discenda* and form a little story.

1. Sīmiam in tabernā videt. _____
2. Sīmia in tabernā sedet. _____
3. "Salvē, sīmia!" paedagōgus inquit. _____
4. "Quid agis?" _____
5. "Habēsne nōmen?" _____
6. Sīmia nihil respondet. _____
7. "Cupisne vīnum?" _____
8. Sīmia pecūniam meam habet. _____
9. Ō sīmia, num pecūniam meam cupis? _____
10. Sīmia ē tabernā currit. _____

05-11 *Verba Discenda*: Latin to English. Select the English match for the Latin word.

1. *ā, ab*____
2. *clāmō* (1) ____
3. *habeō, habēre, habuī, habitum*____
4. *in* (+ abl.) ____
5. *in* (+ acc.) ____
6. *meus, -a, -um*____
7. *num*____
8. *per*____
9. *prope*____
10. *sīmia, -ae* m. ____
11. *ubi*____
12. *via, -ae* f. ____

a. asks a question expecting a "no" answer
b. away from (+ abl.)
c. have, hold
d. in, on, at
e. monkey
f. my
g. near (+ acc.)
h. into
i. road, way
j. shout
k. through (+ acc.)
l. where, when

05-12 *Verba Discenda*: English to Latin. Select the Latin match for the English word.

1. to, toward (+ acc.) ____
2. run ____
3. out of, from (+ abl.) ____
4. city center ____
5. between, among (+ acc.) ____
6. asks a question expecting a "yes" answer ____
7. after, behind (+ acc.) ____
8. sit ____
9. stand ____
10. across (+ acc.) ____

a. *trans*
b. *ad*
c. *stō, stāre, stetī, statum*
d. *nōnne*
e. *sedeō, sedēre, sēdī, sessum*
f. *forum, -ī* n.
g. *inter*
h. *ē, ex*
i. *currō, currere, cucurrī, cursum*
j. *post*

05-13 *Verba Discenda:* **Missing Parts.** Select the answer that supplies the missing information for the dictionary entry for each *Verbum Discendum.* The meaning is not an issue in this exercise.

→ via [viī, *viae*], f.

1. trāns [+ accusative, + ablative]
2. ad [+ accusative, ablative]
3. stō, stāre, [stāvī, stetī]
4. sedeō, [sedere, sedēre]
5. forum, [forī, forae] n.
6. inter [+ accusative, + ablative]
7. ē, ex [+ accusative, + ablative]
8. currō, currere, [cursī, cucurrī], cursum
9. post [+ accusative, + ablative]
10. ā, ab [+ accusative, + ablative]
11. [habeō, habō], habēre, habuī, habitum
12. in = in/on [+ accusative, + ablative]
13. in = into [+ accusative, + ablative]
14. meus, [meī, mea], meum
15. per [+ accusative, + ablative]
16. prope [+ accusative, + ablative]

05-14 **Rome at the Time of Our Story.** Select either V (*vērum*) or F (*falsum*) for each statement.

1. At the time of our story, the Basilica Paulli was being dedicated.	V	F
2. The temple of the Vestals was round.	V	F
3. The *Templum Castorum* was first built in 496 B.C.	V	F
4. Augustus dedicated the *Templum Castorum* in 10 B.C.	V	F
5. The Temple of the Divine Julius was built on the site where he was cremated.	V	F
6. The Vestals had to be virgins.	V	F
7. Vesta was the Goddess of Prosperity.	V	F
8. A public hearth was in the Temple of the Vestals.	V	F
9. Congregations worshipped inside a Roman temple.	V	F
10. Roman temples usually had columns just in front.	V	F

05-15 Crossword Puzzle. Complete the puzzle with information from the chapter.

Across

1 – Relating to cows

3 – "Monkey"

5 – *Habeō*, 2nd principal part

7 – "Trāns"

10 – Word used in a question to expect a "no" answer

12 – Word used in a question to expect a "yes" answer

13 – Most Latin verbs have four _____ parts.

15 – "Where" or "when"

16 – "She wants"

17 – *In* + ablative means "in" or _____

18 – "Per"

19 – Relating to fish

21 – *Poscō*, 3rd principal part

23 – "Out of"

Down

1 – "Inter"

2 – Her priestesses were virgins

4 – Enclitic that is used with a yes/no question

6 – Synonym of *templum*

8 – Greek philosopher with a famously flat nose

9 – Castor's twin brother

11 – Word for a flamboyant burial structure

14 – "Behind"

19 – "Near"

20 – *In* + accusative means _____

22 – *Clāmō*, 3rd principal part

6

In Lūdō Chīrōnis

06-01 Case Endings Review and Update: 1st Declension. Complete the chart of case endings for the 1st declension. The ablative endings are new to this chapter.

Singular

Case	Ending
Nominative	-*a*
1. Genitive	-_____
2. Accusative	-_____
3. Ablative	-_____

Plural

Nominative	-*ae*
4. Genitive	-_____
5. Accusative	-_____
6. Ablative	-_____

06-02 1st Declension Noun Endings. Complete the chart of case endings for the word *fēmina*. The ablative endings are new to this chapter.

Case	**Singular**
Nominative	*fēmina*
1. Genitive	*fēmin*_____
2. Accusative	*fēmin*_____
3. Ablative	*fēmin*_____

	Plural
Nominative	*fēminae*
4. Genitive	*fēmin*_____
5. Accusative	*fēmin*_____
6. Ablative	*fēmin*_____

06-03 Case Endings Review and Update: 2ⁿᵈ Declension. Complete the chart of case endings for the 2ⁿᵈ declension. The ablative endings are new to this chapter.

Singular

Case	Ending
Nominative	*-us, -er, -ir*
1. Genitive	-_____
2. Accusative	-_____
3. Ablative	-_____

Plural

Nominative	*-ī*
4. Genitive	-_____
5. Accusative	-_____
6. Ablative	-_____

06-04 2ⁿᵈ Declension Nouns: Endings. Complete the chart with the correct endings for the word *discipulus*.

Case	**Singular**
Nominative	*discipulus*
Genitive	**1.** *discipul*_____
Accusative	**2.** *discipul*_____
Ablative	**3.** *discipul*_____

	Plural
Nominative	*discipulī*
Genitive	**4.** *discipul*_____
Accusative	**5.** *discipul*_____
Ablative	**6.** *discipul*_____

06-05 2ⁿᵈ Declension Nouns: *vir*. Complete the chart with the correct endings for the word *vir*.

Case	**Singular**
Nominative	*vir*
Genitive	**1.** *vir*_____
Accusative	**2.** *vir*_____
Ablative	**3.** *vir*_____

	Plural
Nominative	*virī*
Genitive	**4.** *vir*_____
Accusative	**5.** *vir*_____
Ablative	**6.** *vir*_____

06-06 2ⁿᵈ Declension Nouns: *magister*. Complete the chart with the correct forms of the word *magister*. Note the stem change.

Case	**Singular**
Nominative	*magister*
Genitive	**1.** *magistr*_____
Accusative	**2.** *magistr*_____
Ablative	**3.** *magistr*_____
	Plural
Nominative	*magistrī*
Genitive	**4.** *magistr*_____
Accusative	**5.** *magistr*_____
Ablative	**6.** *magistr*_____

06-07 Find the Ablatives. Select all the ablatives in the following list.

____ fēminae	____ virī	____ puellās
____ fēminārum	____ familiā	____ puella
____ fēminā	____ familiam	____ puellae
____ fēminās	____ familiīs	____ puerī
____ fēminam	____ familiae	____ puerō
____ vir	____ familiārum	____ puerōs
____ virōs	____ puellam	____ puerōrum
____ virīs	____ puellā	____ puer

06-08 Identifying Endings. The following is a list of nonsense words with a given "declension." Look at the ending and select the answer that tells you which case and number the word could be if it were Latin.

1. blimpiī (2ⁿᵈ declension)
a. nom. sing. and gen. pl.   **b.** gen. sing. and nom. pl.   **c.** nom. pl. only

2. computerā (1ˢᵗ declension)
a. nom. sing. and nom. pl.   **b.** abl. sing. and nom. sing.   **c.** abl. sing. only

3. gagae (1ˢᵗ declension)
a. nom. sing. and gen. pl.   **b.** gen. sing. and nom. pl.   **c.** nom. pl. only

4. accordianō (2ⁿᵈ declension)
a. nom. sing. only   **b.** gen. pl. and abl. pl.   **c.** abl. sing. only

5. telephonīs (2ⁿᵈ declension)
a. gen. sing. and nom. pl.   **b.** abl. pl. and acc. pl.   **c.** abl. pl. only

6. pezās (1ˢᵗ declension)
a. nom. pl. only   **b.** acc. pl. only   **c.** abl. pl. only

06-09 Identifying Case and Number. Select the answer that correctly identifies the case and number of the word in *italics*.

1. Paedagōgus cum *fēminā* breviter confert.
   a. nom. sing.   b. acc. sing.   c. abl. sing.   d. nom. pl.

2. In Valeriae tabernā *fēminae* labōrant.
   a. nom. sing.   b. acc. sing.   c. abl. sing.   d. nom. pl.

3. Licinia pōculum *paedagōgī* aquā implet.
   a. nom. pl.   b. acc. sing.   c. gen. sing.   d. nom. pl.

4. Hermēs pecūniam in *saccīs* habet.
   a. nom. sing.   b. acc. sing.   c. abl. sing.   d. abl. pl.

5. Hermēs aquam cum *vīnō* bibit.
   a. nom. sing.   b. acc. sing.   c. abl. sing.   d. abl. pl.

6. In *Valeriae* tabernā fēminae labōrant.
   a. nom. pl.   b. acc. sing.   c. gen. sing.   d. nom. pl.

7. *Discipulī* in magistrōrum lūdīs sedent.
   a. abl. pl.   b. acc. sing.   c. gen. sing.   d. nom. pl.

8. Hermēs pecūniam magistrī in *saccō* habet.
   a. nom. pl.   b. abl. sing.   c. gen. sing.   d. nom. pl.

06-10 Ablatives: Substitution. Change the **number** of each noun in these prepositional phrases (i.e., change singular to plural or plural to singular). Follow the model.

→ in lūdō   *in lūdīs*

1. cum fēminīs _____
2. dē amīcīs _____
3. ē lūdō _____
4. in tabernā _____
5. in tabulīs _____
6. prō tabernā _____
7. cum ancillīs _____

06-11 Ablatives. For the English word in **bold** in each sentence, provide the proper ablative form of the Latin word in parentheses. Follow the model.

→ Valeria works in the **snack shop** (*taberna*): *tabernā*

1. Socrates lives with **Valeria** (*Valeria*): _____
2. Roman students wrote with styluses on **wax tablets** (*tabula*): _____
3. Roman students walked to school with a **pedagogue** (*paedagōgus*): _____
4. The picture of Chiron on the **tablet** (*tabula*) was not flattering: _____
5. Many teachers work with their **students** (*discipulus*): _____
6. The temple is located in the **Forum** (*Forum*): _____

06-12 Prepositions and Case.

Select the word that correctly fits in the sentence as the object of the preposition.

1. Sōcratēs per _____ currit.
 a. tabernam   **b.** taberna   **c.** tabernā

2. Sōcratēs in _____ est.
 a. via   **b.** viā   **c.** viam

3. Sōcratēs ē _____ currit.
 a. taberna   **b.** tabernam   **c.** tabernā

4. Sōcratēs in _____stat.
 a. arās   **b.** arā   **c.** aram

5. Sōcratēs trans _____ currit.
 a. Forī   **b.** Forum   **c.** Forō

6. Sōcratēs post _____ stat.
 a. paedagōgum   **b.** paedagōgī   **c.** paedagōgō

7. Paedagōgus in (*into*)_____ currit.
 a. basilica   **b.** basilicae   **c.** basilicam

8. Paedagōgus ad _____ currit.
 a. Forum   **b.** Forī   **c.** Forō

06-13 BWIOF.

BWIOF is a way to remember what English prepositions to use when translating an ablative that is not preceded by a preposition. Select the best answer concerning BWIOF.

1. The B in BWIOF stands for:
 a. beneath   **b.** between   **c.** by   **d.** below

2. The W in BWIOF stands for:
 a. without   **b.** within   **c.** with

3. The I in BWIOF stands for:
 a. in   **b.** inside   **c.** into

4. The O in BWIOF stands for:
 a. on   **b.** onto   **c.** over   **d.** of

5. The F in BWIOF stands for:
 a. from   **b.** for   **c.** following

6. You can use BWIOF as an aid if a preposition is before the ablative.
 a. true   **b.** false

06-14 The Verb *Sum*.

Select the right form of *sum* to complete each sentence. Note the words in the *Thēsaurus Verbōrum*.

Thēsaurus Verbōrum

ego I   *tū* you (sing.)   *nōs* (we)   *vōs* you (pl.)

1. Lūcius et Marcus discipulī _____.
 a. est   **b.** es   **c.** sumus   **d.** sunt

2. Ego et tu amīcī (*friends*) _____.
 a. est   **b.** es   **c.** sumus   **d.** sunt

3. Lūcius et vōs in lūdō _____.

   a. est   **b.** estis   **c.** sumus   **d.** sunt

4. Marcus et tū laetī _____.

   a. sunt   **b.** es   **c.** estis   **d.** sumus

5. Valeria et Licinia laetae _____.

   a. sunt   **b.** es   **c.** estis   **d.** sumus

6. Sīmia Sōcratēs in tabernā _____.

   a. es   **b.** est   **c.** sumus   **d.** sunt

7. Tū amīcus meus _____.

   a. es   **b.** est   **c.** sumus   **d.** sunt

8. Ego senātor _____.

   a. est   **b.** sumus   **c.** sum   **d.** sunt

06-15 Derivatives. Many Latin prepositions are used as prefixes in English words. Use the meaning of the English word to identify the translation of the English prefix/Latin preposition (in **bold**). HINT: The English -**ject** comes from the Latin word *iaciō, iacere* meaning "to throw."

1. **in**ject _____   **a.** down

2. **pro**ject _____   **b.** before

3. **de**ject _____   **c.** out

4. **sub**ject _____   **d.** between

5. **e**ject _____   **e.** under

6. **inter**ject _____   **f.** into

06-16 Imperatives. Select the imperatives from this list.

_____ Salvē

_____ Valēte

_____ Ambulat

_____ Da

_____ Disce

_____ Stāte

_____ Tenētis

_____ Scrībitis

_____ Observās

_____ Dūc

_____ Sedē

_____ Fert

_____ Currit

_____ Habēs

_____ Respondēte

_____ Vidē

06-17 Negative Imperatives. Select the properly constructed negative imperatives from this list.

_____ Nōn ambulāre

_____ Nōlī dare

_____ Nōlīte ambulātis

_____ Currite nōn

_____ Nōlīte sedēre

_____ Scrībite

_____ Observā nōn

_____ Nōlī scrībite

_____ Nōlīte vendere

_____ Nōlī currere

06-18 How Closely Did You Read? Select a response for each question or statement.

1. Which what case do you use BWIOF? _____
2. Which case does a preposition generally use to express motion toward? _____
3. Which does the mnemonic MOST MUST ISN'T stand for? _____
4. Which word is used to describe a verbal noun? _____
5. Which mood expresses a direct command in Latin? _____
6. Which Roman poet wrote an epigram about a schoolteacher? _____
7. It's the technical term for freeing a slave. _____
8. He was the Roman emperor who came from Spain. _____
9. It indicates when a person was in his prime. _____
10. Verbs like *ambulat* are in what mood? _____

a. ablative

b. accusative

c. *floruit*

d. imperative

e. indicative

f. infinitive

g. manumission

h. Martial

i. personal endings

j. Trajan

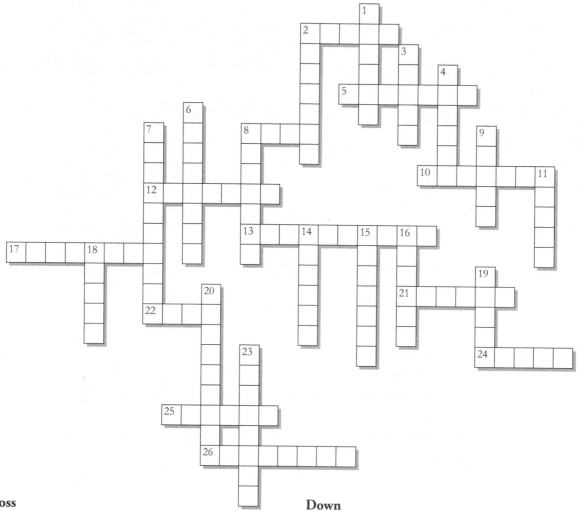

Across

2 – "Boy" (abl. sing.)

5 – Poet born in Spain

8 – "I have made/done"

10 – "Women" (abl. pl.)

12 – "To learn"

13 – A verbal noun

17 – "Teacher" (abl. sing.)

21 – "To hold"

22 – "Without"

24 – "Often"

25 – Lucius' teacher

26 – "To write"

Down

1 – Emperor born in Spain

2 – "Girls" (abl. pl.)

3 – "Y'all are"

4 – "To make/do"

6 – Latin word for a teacher

7 – Latin word for a boy's tutor

8 – "Fl." written out

9 – Your tool for translating solitary ablatives

11 – "Studium"

14 – "He says"

15 – "Sunt"

16 – "Your" *taberna*

18 – "We are"

19 – "Across/over"

20 – Roman name for the Greek god Hermes

23 – "Cras"

7 Post Lūdum

07-01 *Volō, Nōlō, Mālō.* Choose the correct English translation for the following Latin verbs.

1. *vult:*
   a. I want
   b. she wants
   c. they want
   d. you all want

2. *nōlō:*
   a. don't
   b. I don't want
   c. he wants
   d. they want

3. *māvultis:*
   a. he prefers
   b. we prefer
   c. you all prefer
   d. they prefer

4. *possunt:*
   a. he can
   b. they are able
   c. we can
   d. you all are able

5. *nōn vīs:*
   a. he does want
   b. you do not want
   c. they want
   d. you want

6. *potestis:*
   a. you all can
   b. he is able
   c. they can
   d. I can

7. *māvīs*
   a. he prefers
   b. she prefers
   c. we prefer
   d. you prefer

8. *posse:*
   a. to be able
   b. they are able
   c. he is able
   d. I am able

9. *velle:*
   a. wish
   b. I want
   c. to want
   d. he wants

10. *mālunt:*
    a. they want
    b. they prefer
    c. they do not want
    d. he prefers

07-02 Irregular Verbs: *Volō, Nōlō, Mālō, Eō.* Match the correct Latin verb form with the English translation.

1. she can _____
2. you want _____
3. he prefers _____
4. I wish _____
5. I am able _____
6. you don't want _____
7. we prefer _____
8. we are going _____
9. they go _____
10. she doesn't want _____

   a. *īmus*
   b. *mālumus*
   c. *māvult*
   d. *nōn vult*
   e. *nōn vultis*
   f. *possum*
   g. *potest*
   h. *vīs*
   i. *volō*
   j. *eunt*

07-03 The Verb *Eō*. Match the Latin verb with its English translation.

1. *it* _____
2. *eunt* _____
3. *īre* _____
4. *eō* _____
5. *īmus* _____
6. *īs* _____
7. *ī* _____
8. *ītis* _____

a. Go!
b. he/she/it goes
c. I go
d. they go
e. to go
f. we go
g. you (sing.) go
h. you all go

07-04 Four Irregular Verbs: English to Latin. Select the Latin verb that best translates the English.

1. we go
   a. *īmus*   b. *it*   c. *ī*   d. *eō*
2. you (sing.) want
   a. *volō*   b. *vultis*   c. *volumus*   d. *vīs*
3. they (pl.) do not want
   a. *nōlō*   b. *nōn volunt*   c. *vultis*   d. *nōlunt*
4. Go! (sing.).
   a. *īmus*   b. *it*   c. *ī*   d. *īre*
5. we want
   a. *volō*   b. *vultis*   c. *volumus*   d. *vīs*
6. you (pl.) prefer
   a. *magis vultis*   b. *māvultis*   c. *mālumus*   d. *māvīs*
7. you (pl.) do not want
   a. *nōlunt*   b. *nōlō*   c. *nōn vultis* d. *noltis*
8. we prefer
   a. *mālō*   b. *mālumus*   c. *magis volumus* d. *māvīs*
9. we do not want
   a. *nōlumus*   b. *nōn volumus*   c. *nōlimus*   d. *īmus*
10. he prefers
    a. *māvult*   b. *nōn vult*   c. *magis vult* d. *vult*

07-05 Odd One Out. One word in each group does not belong. The answer is never that "it is from a different verb." It may be singular while the others are plural, or 1st person whereas all the others are 2nd. Which ones don't belong? Follow the model.

→ volō, māvultis, nōlō, potest
  māvultis (plural while others are singular)

1. a. volō   b. volumus   c. nōn vultis   d. mālunt
2. a. nōn vultis   b. māvult   c. vīs   d. nōn vult
3. a. possum   b. volumus   c. possunt   d. mālumus
4. a. velle   b. nolī   c. mālle   d. nōlle
5. a. potes   b. māvīs   c. vult   d. possumus
6. a. potes   b. māvīs   c. vultis   d. nōn vīs
7. a. estis   b. volunt   c. possumus   d. māvīs
8. a. potestis   b. potest   c. vīs   d. sum

07-06 3ʳᵈ and 4ᵗʰ Conjugation Verbs: Rules. Complete the following paragraph with information about 3ʳᵈ and 4ᵗʰ conjugation verbs.

The present tense for the 3ʳᵈ and 4ᵗʰ conjugations uses the (1)_____ stem. You find this stem by dropping the (2)_____ of the (3)_____ principal part. Then you add the endings:

-ō   -imus
(4)_____   -itis
(5)_____   (6)_____

Remember . . . i + i = (7)_____.

07-07 3ʳᵈ and 4ᵗʰ Conjugation Verbs: Forms. Select the correct English translation for the Latin verb.

1. capit _____   **a.** I take
2. capis _____   **b.** she seizes
3. audīmus _____   **c.** they lead
4. dūcitis _____   **d.** we hear
5. audītis _____   **e.** you all lead
6. dūcunt _____   **f.** you catch
7. audīs _____   **g.** you all hear
8. capiō _____   **h.** you hear

07-08 3ʳᵈ and 4ᵗʰ Conjugation Verbs: Sentences. Select the form of the verb that will complete the sentence correctly. Note the words in the *Thēsaurus Verbōrum*.

Thēsaurus Verbōrum

ego I	*tū* you (sing.)	*nōs* we	*vōs* you (pl.)
dūcō, dūcere lead	*scrībō, scrībere* write	*dormiō, dormīre* sleep	

1. Lūcius et Marcus _____.
   a. dormit   **b.** dormīs   **c.** dormiunt   **d.** dormīmus
2. Ego et amīcī meī _____.
   a. scrībit   **b.** scrībitis   **c.** scrībimus   **d.** scrībunt
3. Marce, nōnne tū in lūdō _____?
   a. scrībit   **b.** scrībimus   **c.** scrībis   **d.** scrībunt
4. Hermēs Lūcium _____.
   a. dūcis   **b.** dūcit   **c.** dūcitis   **d.** ducunt
5. Hermēs et tū Lūcium _____.
   a. dūcis   **b.** dūcitis   **c.** dūcunt   **d.** dūcimus
6. Sīmia Sōcratēs in tabernā nōn _____.
   a. dormit   **b.** dormīs   **c.** dormiunt   **d.** dormītis
7. Amīcī meī et ego in lūdō _____.
   a. dormīmus   **b.** dormiunt   **c.** dormīs   **d.** dormītis
8. Ego nōn bene _____.
   a. scrībimus   **b.** scrībit   **c.** scrībō   **d.** scrībunt

07-09 3rd and 4th Conjugation Verbs: Creating Forms.

07-09 3rd and 4th Conjugation Verbs: Creating Forms. Fill in the blanks with the correct forms *agō, agere, ēgī, actum* (do, drive) and *dormiō, dormīre, dormīvī* (sleep).

1. you (sing.) sleep   *dorm_____*

2. you all drive   *ag_____*

3. she drives   *ag_____*

4. he is sleeping   *dorm_____*

5. they drive   *ag_____*

6. they sleep   *dorm_____*

7. we drive   *ag_____*

8. we are asleep   *dorm_____*

9. I drive   *ag_____*

10. you all sleep   *dorm_____*

07-10 Forming the Present Tense: All Conjugations.

07-10 Forming the Present Tense: All Conjugations. Use the principal parts in parentheses to determine the conjugation of the verb, then select the correct Latin translation of the English prompt.

1. he calls (*vocō, vocāre*)

  a. *vocet*   **b.** *vocat*   **c.** *vocit*   **d.** *vocēt*

2. he warns (*moneō, monēre*)

  a. *monet*   **b.** *monat*   **c.** *monit*   **d.** *monēt*

3. they say (*dīcō, dīcere*)

  a. *dīciunt*   **b.** *dīcant*   **c.** *dīcunt*   **d.** *dīcēnt*

4. they hear (*audiō , audīre*)

  a. *audent*   **b.** *audunt*   **c.** *audiunt*   **d.** *audēnt*

5. I owe (*dēbeō, dēbēre*)

  a. *dēbō*   **b.** *dēbeō*   **c.** *dēbēō*   **d.** *dēbiō*

6. you laugh (*rīdeō, rīdēre*)

  a. *rīdeas*   **b.** *rīdēs*   **c.** *rīdis*   **d.** *rīdas*

7. she learns (*discō, discere*)

  a. *discit*   **b.** *discet*   **c.** *discēt*   **d.** *discat*

8. we write (*scrībō, scrībere*)

  a. *scrībamus*   **b.** *scrībēmus*   **c.** *scrībimus*   **d.** *scribemus*

9. they do (*faciō, facere*)

  a. *facent*   **b.** *faciunt*   **c.** *facunt*   **d.** *facēnt*

10. you all take (*capiō, capere*)

  a. *capetis*   **b.** *capatis*   **c.** *capietis*   **d.** *capitis*

Name: _____   Date: _____

07-11 Forming 3rd and 4th Conjugation Verbs. The "Stem" column of the table contains a short present stem. Add any one of the endings below to that stem, make a form, and translate it. Remember: "i + i = i." Use each of the six endings at least once. Follow the model.

	Singular	**Plural**
1st	ō	imus
2nd	is	itis
3rd	it	unt

Stem	**Ending**	**Form**	**Translation**
→ curr-	-is	curris	you run
1. ag-	_____	_____	_____
2. bib-	_____	_____	_____
3. capi-	_____	_____	_____
4. dīc-	_____	_____	_____
5. disc-	_____	_____	_____
6. dūc-	_____	_____	_____
7. faci-	_____	_____	_____
8. posc-	_____	_____	_____
9. scrīb-	_____	_____	_____
10. veni-	_____	_____	_____

07-12 3rd and 4th Conjugation Verbs. Select the best English translation for the Latin verb form.

1. *age* _____
2. *audiunt* _____
3. *bibere* _____
4. *capimus* _____
5. *capit* _____
6. *currunt* _____
7. *dīc* _____
8. *discite* _____
9. *dūcis* _____
10. *faciunt* _____
11. *bibe* _____
12. *pōnunt* _____
13. *poscitis* _____
14. *scrībunt* _____
15. *venīmus* _____
16. *dormīs* _____

a. drink!
b. drive!
c. learn!
d. she is seizing
e. speak!
f. they are doing
g. they hear
h. they run
i. they write
j. they put
k. to drink
l. we are coming
m. we seize
n. you are leading
o. you ask for
p. you sleep

07-13 Irregular Verbs: Volō. Complete the chart to produce the present tense of *volō*.

	Singular	Plural
1st person	*volō*	*volumus*
2nd person	1. _____	3. _____
3rd person	2. _____	4. _____

07-14 Irregular Verbs: Nōlō. Complete the chart to produce the present tense of *nōlō*.

	Singular	Plural
1st person	*nōlō*	*nōlumus*
2nd person	1. _____	3. _____
3rd person	2. _____	4. _____

07-15 Irregular Verbs: Mālō. Complete the chart to produce the present tense of *mālō*.

	Singular	Plural
1st person	*mālō*	*mālumus*
2nd person	1. _____	3. _____
3rd person	2. _____	4. _____

07-16 Compound Forms of Eō. Use your knowledge of prepositions to select the English that seems best to translate the compound form of *eō*. One will be a surprise.

1. *adeō* _____
2. *ineō* _____
3. *pereō* _____
4. *transeō* _____
5. *abeō* _____
6. *circumeō* _____

a. approach
b. die, perish
c. enter
d. go across
e. go around
f. go away from

07-17 How Closely Did You Read? Match each term with its identification.

1. *lībertīnus* _____
2. Antioch on the Orontes _____
3. Silk Road _____
4. *pilleus lībertātis* _____
5. *nōlī mē tangere* _____
6. complementary infinitive _____
7. Publilius Syrus _____
8. *nōlle prōsequī* _____
9. *nōlō contendere* _____
10. manumission _____

a. special cap worn by a newly freed Roman slave
b. author of *Sententiae* (*The Sentences* or *Proverbs*), a collection of Latin maxims
c. a plea where the accused decides not to contest the charge, instead of admitting guilt
d. refers to a type of painting
e. process of a Roman master releasing his slave
f. used in law to refer to a plaintiff or prosecutor's decision not to pursue a case
g. used with words like *possum* and *volō* to complete their meaning
h. City in Roman Syria
i. Latin word for a freed slave
j. ran from the Roman province of Syria to China

07-18 Crossword Puzzle. Complete the puzzle with information from the chapter.

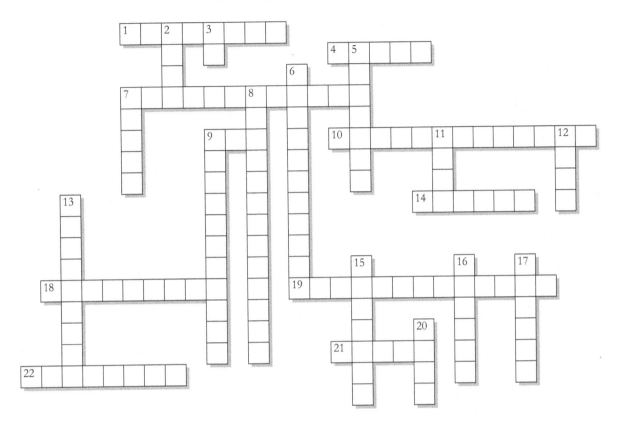

Across

1 – "Lībertīnus"

4 – "You (sing.) prefer"

7 – "Please"

9 – Stem of *possum*

10 – Kind of infinitive found after *volō*, *nōlō*, etc.

14 – *Sī vīs pacem, parā* _____

18 – The praenomen of a Syrian author of mimes

19 – A type of religious painting

21 – "I ought to"

22 – "We are able"

Down

2 – "They go"

3 – "Down from, concerning"

5 – Major Syrian city

6 – The process of freeing a slave

7 – The Spanish verb "estar" comes from this Latin verb

8 – The head of a Roman family

9 – Most singular imperatives are identical to this

11 – "To eat" (infinitive form)

12 – 3rd principal part of *rīdeō*

13 – "Y'all don't want to"

15 – Special cap worn by freed slaves

16 – A major vegetable crop from Syria

17 – "Amīcus"

20 – There are _____ conjugations in Latin

8 Eāmus Domum!

08-01 Vocatives. Select the correct Latin vocative for the English word in **bold** in the sentence.

1. **Marcus**, could you come over here, please?
   a. Marcus   b. Marce   c. Marcī

2. Listen up! **Lucius**, you are going first.
   a. Lūcie   b. Lūcius   c. Lūcī   d. Lūc

3. Oh, **Flavia**, I need three figs right away!
   a. Flāvia   b. Flāvie   c. Flāviae

4. You **maid servants**, come help your mistress with her hair.
   a. ancilla   b. ancillae   c. ancillā   d. ancille

5. Chiron shouted, "**Boys**! Back to your seats!"
   a. puerī   b. puere   c. puer

6. The boys replied, "Yes, **master**."
   a. magistre   b. magistrī   c. magister

7. Servilius turned to the slave and said, "You, **boy**, get to work."
   a. puerī   b. puere   c. puer

8. Caecilia said, "**Servilia**, we must hurry before it rains."
   a. Servīlie   b. Servīliae   c. Servīlia

9. Lucius asked Hermes, "**My pedagogue**, could we go home now?"
   a. me paedagōge b. mī paedagōgī c. meus paedagōgus   d. mī paedagōge

10. Servilius smiled and said, "**My sons**, I will never forget this."
    a. mī filī   b. me filie   c. meī filiī   d. mī filiī

08-02 Forming Perfects: The Formula. Fill in the blanks to create the formula for making every perfect tense in the Latin language. The answers are in the *Thēsaurus Verbōrum*, but not every word in the *Thēsaurus Verbōrum* is used.

Thēsaurus Verbōrum

1st	-*it*
2nd	perfect
3rd	present
-*ērunt*	short present
-*ī*	-*vī*

Take the (1)_____ stem, found by dropping the (2)_____ of the (3)_____ principal part.

To this stem add the endings:

	Singular	Plural
1st person	___-*ī*___	(6)_____
3rd person	(4)_____	(5)_____

08-03 Identifying Perfects.
Select each verb that is in the perfect tense. All are in the 3rd person, so you have to concentrate on the stem.

_____	ambulat	_____	respondent
_____	ambulāvit	_____	respondērunt
_____	cōgitant	_____	surgunt
_____	cōgitāvērunt	_____	surrexērunt
_____	dūcit	_____	venit
_____	dūxit	_____	vēnit
_____	est	_____	voluit
_____	fuit	_____	vult

08-04 Perfect Endings: English to Latin.
Select the ending that the verb in **bold** would have if it were in Latin. All are perfect tense endings. Follow the model.

→ __c__ Aelius **finished** his work hours ago.

a. -it   **b.** -ērunt

1. They **went** there last year.

a. -it   **b.** -ērunt

2. Aelius and Licinia **met** in Rome.

a. -it   **b.** -ērunt

3. Licinia and Aelius **had** lots of work today.

a. -it   **b.** -ērunt

4. The soldiers I **have done** that many times already.

a. -it   **b.** -ērunt

5. Flavia once **lived** in Germany.

a. -it   **b.** -ērunt

6. **Have** the senators **travelled** from far away?

a. -it   **b.** -ērunt

08-05 3rd Principal Part Practice.
Select the correct translation for the Latin word. Note that all the Latin words are 3rd principal parts of *Verba Discenda*.

1. ambulāvī _____		**a.**	I drove
2. audīvī _____		**b.**	I gave
3. cēpī _____		**c.**	I have been
4. cucurrī _____		**d.**	I heard
5. dedī _____		**e.**	I led
6. dīxī _____		**f.**	I made
7. dūxī _____		**g.**	I ran
8. ēgī _____		**h.**	I said
9. fēcī _____		**i.**	I took
10. fuī _____		**j.**	I walked

08-06 Perfect Tense: Plural to Singular. Change the number of the following plural perfect forms, making them singular without changing the person. Follow the model.

→ labōrāvērunt   *labōrāvit*

1. intrāvērunt   _____
2. īvērunt   _____
3. māluērunt   _____
4. cucurrērunt   _____
5. cupīvērunt   _____
6. dēbuērunt   _____

08-07 Perfect Tense: Singular to Plural. Change the number of the following singular perfect forms, making them plural without changing the person. Follow the model.

→ posuit   *posuērunt*

1. dedit   _____
2. didicit   _____
3. dīxit   _____
4. dūxit   _____
5. poposcit   _____
6. portāvit   _____

08-08 Perfect Tense: Changing the Number. Change the number of the following perfect forms, making them singular if they are plural and plural if they are singular. Do not change the person.

1. potuit   _____
2. rīsit   _____
3. salūtāvērunt   _____
4. sēdērunt   _____

08-09 Translating Perfects and Presents. Select the correct translation for each verb form.

1. *habuit*
   a. he has   **b.** he had
2. *potest*
   a. he is able   **b.** he has been able
3. *venīt*
   a. he is coming   **b.** he came
4. *vīdet*
   a. he sees   **b.** he saw

08-10 Expressions of Time: Case Use.
Given the rules for the use of the ablative and accusative in expressions of time, what case would you use to express the English word(s) in **bold** in Latin?

1. Aelius goes to his shop every day **at daybreak**.
  a. ablative   **b.** accusative

2. He works **ten hours** a day.
  a. ablative   **b.** accusative

3. At **noon** he goes home for lunch.
  a. ablative   **b.** accusative

4. After lunch he takes a siesta and sleeps **for one hour**.
  a. ablative   **b.** accusative

5. **During the two hours** he is gone, his slave Hephaestus also sleeps.
  a. ablative   **b.** accusative

6. Aelius has been doing this **for three years**.
  a. ablative   **b.** accusative

7. **During the summer** it gets very hot near the forge.
  a. ablative   **b.** accusative

8. **On the day** his baby is born he will not go to work.
  a. ablative   **b.** accusative

08-11 Expressions of Time.
From the *Thēsaurus Verbōrum*, select the appropriate Latin word for each of the English expressions of time marked in **bold** in the following paragraph. Not all the words in the *Thēsaurus* are used, and none is used twice.

Thēsaurus Verbōrum

annīs	*hōrā*	*merīdiē*
annōs	*hōram*	*merīdiem*
annum	*hōrās*	

At the fifth **hour** (1)_____ Aelius stepped away from his forge. He had been working for six **hours** (2)_____ straight. Soon, at **midday** (3)_____ he could break and take some lunch. He had been running his little shop for four **years** (4)_____ now, and business was good.

08-12 Comprehension.
The following sentences ask questions based on events in *Lectiō Prīma*. Find the answer to the question in the *lectiō* and write it below the English as a complete Latin sentence. Follow the model.

→ Quid Lūcius et Hermēs in viā vident?
  Lectīcam ornātam in viā vident.

1. Quis (who?) prō lectīcā ambulat? _____

2. Quis post lectīcam ambulat? _____

3. Quid in terrā servī pōnunt? _____

4. Ubi servī stant? _____

5. Quid Servīlia mox facere oportet? _____

6. Cūr servī nōn laetī sunt? _____

08-13 *Verba Discenda:* **Derivatives.** Fill in the blanks with the Latin *Verbum Discendum* from which the English word in **bold** ultimately derives. You do not have to list the entire dictionary listing for the Latin word.

1. As **negotiations** stalled, both sides became irritated. _____

2. Lewis turned to Clark and said, "We'll never cross the river here. We have to find a place of **portage**." _____

3. Since the **entrance** was blocked, we went around to the side. _____

4. His amateur magic was fun at first, but soon the **novelty** wore off. _____

5. Be careful, my patience is not **infinite**. _____

6. I don't like the **consistency** of this pudding. _____

7. Your honor, I'd like to **invoke** the Fifth Amendment. _____

8. When in Chicago, I like to shop on the **Magnificent** Mile. _____

08-14 *Verba Discenda.* Match the *Verbum Discendum* with its English meaning.

1. *ancilla, -ae* f. _____   **a.** beyond
2. *ergō* _____   **b.** also
3. *fessus, -a, -um* _____   **c.** task
4. *filia, -ae* f. _____   **d.** call
5. *finiō, finīre, finīvī/finiī, finītum* _____   **e.** carry
6. *hōra, -ae* f. _____   **f.** daughter
7. *iam* _____   **g.** female servant
8. *magnus, -a, -um* _____   **h.** finish
9. *negōtium, -iī* n. _____   **i.** hour
10. *novus, -a, -um* _____   **j.** land
11. *portō* (1) _____   **k.** great
12. *praeter* (+ acc.) _____   **l.** new
13. *quoque* _____   **m.** now
14. *sēdecim* _____   **n.** sixteen
15. *sistō, sistere, stetī/stitī, statum* _____   **o.** stand still
16. *terra, -ae* f. _____   **p.** therefore
17. *vocō* (1) _____   **q.** tired

08-15 How Closely Did You Read? Select the correct word or phrase for each clue.

1. The open, flat area north and west of the Capitoline Hill where the Romans mustered troops and voting citizens. _____

2. A Latin expression that means "Seize the day." _____

3. The Latin expression used by Cicero to lament the bad state of affairs in Rome. _____

4. This case is used to make a direct address. _____

5. The Latin word for "clock." _____

6. A grammatical term that indicates the time and kind of action of a verb. _____

7. Form of a Latin verb translated into English as "_____-ed" or "has _____-ed". _____

8. Park in which Augustus erected an Egyptian obelisk as the arm of a sun dial. _____

9. A Latin phrase used today for a daily expense allowance. _____

10. Construction used to show the time at which an action took place. _____

11. Construction used to show how long an action lasted. _____

12. A Latin phrase describing the quick passage of time. _____

a. Ablative of Time Within Which
b. Accusative of Extent of Time
c. *Campus Martius*
d. *Carpe diem*
e. *Hōrologium*
f. *Ō tempora, ō mōrēs!*
g. *Per diem*
h. Perfect tense
i. *Sōlārium Augustī*
j. *Tempus fugit*
k. Tense
l. Vocative

08-16 Crossword Puzzle. Complete the puzzle with information from the chapter.

Across

3 – "Therefore"

8 – "Maid servant"

10 – Latin word for sundial

12 – Romans divided the day into 12 of these

13 – Romans divided nighttime into 4 of these

16 – "To stand still"

18 – Vocative sing. of "Marcus"

19 – "To enter"

20 – "Time flies"

22 – "Also"

Down

1 – "Land"

2 – Case used when addressing someone

4 – "Negōtium"

5 – The official, religious boundary of Rome

6 – Romans voted here

7 – Vocative sing. of "Lucius"

9 – "Seize the day"

11 – Vocative sing. of "filius"

14 – Latin word for a water clock

15 – Vocative of "magister"

17 – Slaves carried Romans in one of these

21 – "Tired" (masc.)

9   Per Viās Rōmānās

09-01 Identifying Genitive Phrases. Find the genitive in the following sentences from *Lectiō Prīma*. If an adjective modifies the genitive noun, select it also. Then find the word with which the genitive is linked. Follow the model.

	Genitive	Linked With
→ Plūs negōtiī nōn in Forō est.	*negōtiī*	*plūs*
1. Labor fēminārum in tabernā fīnīvit.	_____	_____
2. Familia Valeriae habitat in Subūrā.	_____	_____
3. Tonsor, vir magnae statūrae, prō tabernā stetit.	_____	_____
4. Tonsor virum parvae statūrae rāsit.	_____	_____
5. "Quid novī, amīce?"	_____	_____
6. Fortasse aliquis malī animī nostra verba audit.	_____	_____

09-02 Review of Genitive Forms. Select the word that represents the correct Latin for the English word or phrase in **bold**.

1. Hermes is carrying a sack **of money**.
   a. *pecūniam*   **b.** *pecūniae*

2. After school Chiron cleans the **boys'** tablets.
   a. *puerī*   **b.** *puerōrum*

3. **Licinia's** apartment house is in the Subura.
   a. *Liciniae*   **b.** *Licinia*

4. The beds of the **maid servants** are crowded into one room.
   a. *ancillae*   **b.** *ancillārum*

5. The barber sees that the **man's** beard is tough.
   a. *virōrum*   **b.** *virī*

6. **Teachers'** pay in Rome was not very high.
   a. *magistrōrum*   **b.** *magistrī*

09-03 Genitive of Possession: Concept. Write three sentences in English illustrating the genitive of possession. Follow the model.

→ I just heard about the President's speech.

1. _____

2. _____

3. _____

09-04 Genitive of Description: Concept. Write three sentences in English illustrating the genitive of description. Follow the model.

→ Winnie the Pooh always says he is a bear of little brain.

1. _____
2. _____
3. _____

09-05 Partitive Genitive (Genitive of the Whole): Concept. Write three sentences in English illustrating the partitive genitive. Follow the model.

→ A small number of the men ran away during the battle.

1. _____
2. _____
3. _____

09-06 Identifying Uses of the Genitive in English. Select the correct use of the genitive as exemplified by the words in **bold** in the English sentence.

1. **Part of me** wants to run, the other wants to stay.
   a. genitive of possession   **b.** genitive of description   **c.** partitive genitive

2. **Julia Child's** cookbook is my favorite.
   a. genitive of possession   **b.** genitive of description   **c.** partitive genitive

3. **My team's** record this year is terrible.
   a. genitive of possession   **b.** genitive of description   **c.** partitive genitive

4. There isn't even a hint **of deception** in the suspect, Captain.
   a. genitive of possession   **b.** genitive of description   **c.** partitive genitive

5. Well, Sergeant, I disagree. I think he is a man **of low morals**.
   a. genitive of possession   **b.** genitive of description   **c.** partitive genitive

6. Groucho was the funniest **of the Marx Brothers**.
   a. genitive of possession   **b.** genitive of description   **c.** partitive genitive

09-07 Phrase Analysis in Latin: The Genitive. Select the correct use of the genitive as exemplified by the Latin phrase in ***bold italics***.

1. *Videō actōrēs **magnī ingeniī**.*
   a. genitive of possession   **b.** genitive of description   **c.** partitive genitive

2. *Videō nōnnullōs virōs **paucae industriae**.*
   a. genitive of possession   **b.** genitive of description   **c.** partitive genitive

3. *Audiō ancillās **Servīliī**.*
   a. genitive of possession   **b.** genitive of description   **c.** partitive genitive

4. *Videō **dominārum** lectīcās.*
   a. genitive of possession   **b.** genitive of description   **c.** partitive genitive

5. *Servīlia in aliā **viae** parte est.*
   a. genitive of possession   **b.** genitive of description   **c.** partitive genitive

6. ***Servīliī** servī nōn laetī sunt.*
   a. genitive of possession   **b.** genitive of description   **c.** partitive genitive

09-08 Genitive Phrases. Combine a non-genitive word with a genitive phrase to make six genitive phrases, two of each type: Genitive of Possession, Genitive of Description, Genitive of the Whole. Then translate each phrase you make into idiomatic English. Words may be used more than once. Follow the models.

aliquid (something, a bit)	*Liciniae*
fēmina	*fābulārum*
filiās	*bonī animī*
forum	*virōrum Rōmānōrum*
multum (a great deal)	*magnī pretiī* (of great price)
paedagōgōs	*multōrum verbōrum* (of many words)
pars (part)	*magnae industriae* (of great diligence)
plus	*nōn magnae industriae*
puer	*paucī spatiī* (of little space)
taberna	*pecūniae*
vir	*multae pecūniae*
virī	*Valeriae*

Type	Phrase	Translation
→ Possession	Valeriae taberna	Valeria's snack shop
→ Description	taberna magnī spatiī	a shop with lots of space (a shop of great space)
→ Whole	aliquid pecūniae	a bit of money (something of money)
1. Possession	_____	_____
2. Possession	_____	_____
3. Description	_____	_____
4. Description	_____	_____
5. Whole	_____	_____
6. Whole	_____	_____

09-09 Possessive Adjectives. Select the word that you would use to translate the English word in **bold** into Latin. Don't worry about any agreements here.

1. George, get **your** mongoose out of the living room!
   a. *tuus*   **b.** *meus*   **c.** *noster*   **d.** *vester*   **e.** *suus*

2. I'll move it into **my** bedroom, how's that?
   a. *tuus*   **b.** *meus*   **c.** *noster*   **d.** *vester*   **e.** *suus*

3. Your father and I will not have that thing in **our** house!
   a. *tuus*   **b.** *meus*   **c.** *noster*   **d.** *vester*   **e.** *suus*

4. But Charley has one in **his** house!
   a. *tuus*   **b.** *meus*   **c.** *noster*   **d.** *vester*   **e.** *suus*

5. If the Johnsons want to have a mongoose in **their** house, that is their business.
   a. *tuus*   **b.** *meus*   **c.** *noster*   **d.** *vester*   **e.** *suus*

6. OK. But for tonight can I put it in **your** bedroom, Mom and Dad?
   a. *tuus*   **b.** *meus*   **c.** *noster*   **d.** *vester*   **e.** *suus*

09-10 Translating *suus, -a, -um*. Use the subject of each sentence to determine which meaning of *suus, -a, -um* (in **bold**) best fits the context.

1. *Servus dominī **suī** magnam arcam portat.*
   a. his own   **b.** her own   **c.** their own

2. *Servī magnam arcam dominī **suī** portant.*
   a. his own   **b.** her own   **c.** their own

3. *Ancillae magnam arcam dominārum **suārum** portat.*
   a. his own   **b.** her own   **c.** their own

4. *Licinia et Lūcius cum amīcō **suō** ambulant.*
   a. his own   **b.** her own   **c.** their own

5. *Lūcius cum amīcā **suā** ambulat.*
   a. his own   **b.** her own   **c.** their own

6. *Licinia cum amīcīs **suīs** ambulat.*
   a. his own   **b.** her own   **c.** their own

7. *Lūcius cum amīcīs **suīs** ambulat.*
   a. his own   **b.** her own   **c.** their own

8. *Licinia cum amīcā **suā** ambulat.*
   a. his own   **b.** her own   **c.** their own

09-11 Translating *suus, -a, -um*. Translate each sentence in a way that shows you understand how *suus, -a, -um* translates into English. You may omit the word "own." Follow the model.

→ Fēmina Rōmāna puerōs suōs semper amat.
   A Roman woman always loves her children.

1. Sōcratēs domum suam amat. _____

2. Fēminae Rōmānae domum suam semper amant. _____

3. Pater nōn semper servōs suōs amat. _____

4. Māter puellam suam nōn videt. _____

5. Puellae ancillās suās nōn vident. _____

6. Marcus amīcōs suōs ad lūdum vocat. _____

7. Marcus et Lūcius amīcum suum ad lūdum vocant. _____

8. Puerī sīmiam suum amant. _____

09-12 Comprehension: *Lectiōnēs Prīma et Secunda*. Select the correct answer to each question.

1. Ubi familia Valeriae habitat? _____   **a.** fābula Plautī

2. Ubi Valeria et Licinia multa varia vidērunt? _____   **b.** in fullōnicā

3. Quid est *Amphitryō*? _____   **c.** in Subūrā

4. Quid virī in viā iaciunt? _____   **d.** āleās

5. Ubi tonsor virum parvae statūrae rāsit? _____   **e.** in angulō viae

6. Quis pila lūdit? _____   **f.** prō tabernā suā

7. Quid fullō ūrīnā purgit? _____   **g.** tunicās et togās et omnia alia vestīmenta

8. Ubi fullō labōrat? _____   **h.** puerī

Name: _____ **Date:** _____

09-13 *Verba Discenda:* **Derivatives.** Based on the meanings of the *Verba Discenda*, choose the probable meaning of the English words.

1. alias ____
2. audacity ____
3. audible ____
4. collaboration ____
5. conspectus ____
6. nostrum ____

a. a general overview of something
b. a secret, special cure that is ours alone
c. able to be heard
d. another name someone uses
e. boldness
f. the act of working with someone

09-14 **How Carefully Did You Read?** Match the term with the Latin word or phrase that best fits.

1. genitive of the whole ____
2. genitive of description ____
3. reflexive adjective ____
4. let the buyer beware ____
5. Roman laundry ____
6. neighborhood of Rome ____

a. *virōs industriae* (men of diligence)
b. *plūs negōtiī* (more of business = more business)
c. *caveat emptor*
d. *fullōnica*
e. *Subūra*
f. *suus, -a, -um*

09-15 Crossword Puzzle. Complete the puzzle using information from the chapter.

Across

1 – Ancient laundry
2 – "I have heard"
5 – Latin for an apartment block
7 – "____ *virumque canō*"
8 – "A man of great influence" is an example of a genitive of ____
11 – "Noster"
13 – "Let the buyer beware"
16 – "Your" (for one person)
17 – "To hasten"
18 – "Your" (for more than one person)
19 – "On account of"

Down

1 – "Story, play"
3 – The hill on which Servilius lives
4 – "Laundryman"
6 – "Another"
7 – "To dare"
9 – Licinia's home is in this neighborhood
10 – "In front of"
12 – "Valeria's monkey" is an example of a genitive of ____
14 – "To lose"
15 – "My"

10   Quantī Id Constat?

10-01 Dative Endings. Select the Latin word that represents the correct dative form for the English word in **bold**.

1. The grocer gave the five eggs **to Valeria**.
   - **a.** *Valeria*
   - **b.** *Valeriā*
   - **c.** *Valeriae*

2. She took them home, made dinner, and served it to her **family**.
   - **a.** *familiae*
   - **b.** *familia*
   - **c.** *familiā*

3. Licinia had a little bit left over and gave it to **Aelius**.
   - **a.** *Aeliī*
   - **b.** *Aelium*
   - **c.** *Aeliō*

4. The next day, at his forge, Aelius made toys for parents to give their **sons**.
   - **a.** *filiō*
   - **b.** *filiīs*
   - **c.** *filiī*

5. Nearby, a delivery man was giving his **horse** some hay.
   - **a.** *equī*
   - **b.** *equīs*
   - **c.** *equō*

6. Rich people gave their **horses** oats.
   - **a.** *equī*
   - **b.** *equīs*
   - **c.** *equō*

10-02 Indirect Objects: English. Select all the indirect objects in this little story. Be careful! Every use of "to" with a noun or pronoun does not mean there is an indirect object. Sometimes it indicates the preposition *ad* + the accusative or an infinitive.

Servilius gave his manager some money and told him to go to his estate in the country. There he was to buy twenty chickens and three pigs, give them to the cooks, and have them prepare a feast. In two days Servilius would present a banquet to his friends. Next he gave a slave some invitations to deliver and added strict orders to be back in two hours. The slave ran quickly, handed each person his invitation, and returned quickly.

10-03 Identifying Datives. Select each word from the list that can be dative case, singular or plural.

_____ virī

_____ virō

_____ virōs

_____ vīnīs

_____ vīna

_____ puellam

_____ puellae

_____ puellīs

_____ puellā

_____ puellās

10-04 Using Datives. Choose the correct dative form to complete each sentence.

1. Venditor _____ quattuor ōva dedit.
   a. Lūcius   b. Lūciī   c. Lūciō   d. Lūcium

2. Haec ōva _____ praestant.
   a. alium ōvum   b. aliīs ōvīs   c. alia ōva

3. Fēminae emere _____ aliqua voluērunt.
   a. virōrum   b. virī   c. virōs   d. virīs

4. Valeria _____ duōs nummōs dedit.
   a. discipulus   b. discipulī   c. discipulōs   d. discipulō

5. Nunc virī _____ appropinquāvērunt.
   a. fēminīs   b. fēminās   c. fēminārum   d. fēminā

6. Lūcius _____ sīmiam emit.
   a. Servīlia   b. Servīliam   c. Servīliā   d. Servīliae

10-05 Dative, Genitive, or Nominative Plural? In the 1ˢᵗ declension, the genitive singular, dative singular, and nominative plural look alike. But context generally avoids confusion. Choose whether each word in **bold** is genitive or dative singular or nominative plural.

1. *Valeria **ancillae** cibum dat.*
   a. dative singular   b. genitive singular   c. nominative plural

2. *Valeria **Caeciliae** servō cibum dat.*
   a. dative singular   b. genitive singular   c. nominative plural

3. *Valeria **Caeciliae** ancillās dat.*
   a. dative singular   b. genitive singular   c. nominative plural

4. ***Ancillae** Caeciliae ad Forum ambulant.*
   a. dative singular   b. genitive singular   c. nominative plural

5. *Aelius tabernae **Valeriae** appropinquat.*
   a. dative singular   b. genitive singular   c. nominative plural

6. *Ancillae Germānicae **Caeciliae** idōneae sunt.*
   a. dative singular   b. genitive singular   c. nominative plural

7. ***Ancillae** Germānicae Caeciliae idōneae sunt.*
   a. dative singular   b. genitive singular   c. nominative plural

8. *Ancillae **Germānicae** Caeciliae idōneae sunt.*
   a. dative singular   b. genitive singular   c. nominative plural

9. *Ancillae Germānicae Caeciliae **idōneae** sunt.*
   a. dative singular   b. genitive singular   c. nominative plural

10. *Ancillae **Caeciliae** appropinquant.*
    a. dative singular   b. genitive singular   c. nominative plural

10-06 Dative or Ablative Plural? In every declension the dative and ablative plural look alike. But context generally helps avoid confusion. Choose whether each word in **bold** is dative or ablative plural.

1. Fēmina cum **puerīs** ad Forum ambulat.
   a. dative plural   **b.** ablative plural

2. Fēmina **puerīs** pecūniam paucam dat.
   a. dative plural   **b.** ablative plural

3. Fēmina **nummīs** cibum ēmit.
   a. dative plural   **b.** ablative plural

4. Chīrōn prō **discipulīs** stat.
   a. dative plural   **b.** ablative plural

5. Chīrōn **discipulīs** tabulās dat.
   a. dative plural   **b.** ablative plural

6. Chīrōn **discipulīs** appropinquat.
   a. dative plural   **b.** ablative plural

7. Haec ōva **aliīs** praestant.
   a. dative plural   **b.** ablative plural

8. Marcus **Servīliae** adesse vult.
   a. dative plural   **b.** ablative plural

10-07 Comprehension: *Lectiō Prīma.* Use *Lectiō Prīma* to answer each question. Answer in a complete Latin sentence. Follow the model.

→ What did the women approach at the beginning of the narrative?
   Nunc fēminae macellō appropinquāvērunt.

1. What animals are standing near the grocery store? _____

2. What are the dogs doing? _____

3. How much does the merchant say the vegetables cost? _____

4. How much does the grocer say six eggs cost? _____

5. How many coins does Valeria give the grocer for her second purchase? _____

6. At the end of negotiations, what does Valeria buy from the grocer? _____

10-08 Neuters. Select all the neuter nouns in this passage. Use both endings and context to help you find them. If a word is used more than once, select it each time.

Valeria ōva et vīnum ēmit. Tunc ad dēlūbrum fēminae prōcessērunt. In dēlūbrō astrologus oleum super aquam effūdit et fātum puerī prōnuntiāvit (*announced*). Fēminae laetae duo ōva in dēlūbrō posuērunt.

10-09 Recognizing Neuters.

Sometimes if you don't know a word's gender, context and logic can help. Determine whether the word marked in **bold** must be neuter or not. All the sentences are based on *Lectiō Secunda*. Follow the models.

→ *Valeria duo **ōva** habet.*
   a. Yes, it must be neuter. (It is obviously the direct object and accusative; only neuter plurals end in -*a*).

→ *Valeria ūnum **ōvum** habet.*
   b. No, it doesn't have to be neuter. (It is obviously the direct object and accusative, but the ending -*um* is also accusative for 2nd declension masculines).

1. *Fēminae multa **animālia** vident.*
   a. Yes, it must be neuter.   **b.** No, it doesn't have to be neuter.

2. *Virī nōn **ossa** edunt.*
   a. Yes, it must be neuter.   **b.** No, it doesn't have to be neuter.

3. ***Ōvum** antīquum est.*
   a. Yes, it must be neuter.   **b.** No, it doesn't have to be neuter.

4. *Volō **oleum** emere.*
   a. Yes, it must be neuter.   **b.** No, it doesn't have to be neuter.

5. ***Animālia** ubīque sunt!*
   a. Yes, it must be neuter.   **b.** No, it doesn't have to be neuter.

6. *Fēminae **pōmum** spectāvērunt.*
   a. Yes, it must be neuter.   **b.** No, it doesn't have to be neuter.

10-10 Neuters: Singular to Plural.

Complete each sentence with the plural form of the neuter nouns in parentheses. Follow the model.

→ Sīmia per _____ (forum) cucurrit.
   Sīmia per *fora* cucurrit.

1. Fēminae ad _____ (dēlūbrum) vēnērunt.

2. Nunc fēminae _____ (macellō) appropinquāvērunt.

3. Venditor Valeriae _____ (ōvum) dedit.

4. Astrologus _____ (oleum) super aquam effūdit.

5. Virō suō omnia dē _____ (verbō) astrologī narrāre voluit.

6. Post _____ (macellum) canēs ossa edunt.

10-11 Numbers.

Answer the following mathematical problems in Latin by writing out the word required. Follow the model.

→ Ūnum et ūnum sunt *duo*

1. Duo et ūnum sunt _____

2. Duo et duo sunt _____

3. Duo et tria sunt _____

4. Tria et ūnum sunt _____

5. Tria et tria sunt _____

6. Ūnum et tria et duo sunt _____

7. Duo et duo et duo sunt _____

10-12 Declension Review. Indicate all the forms each word can represent. Do not consider the vocative. Use the abbreviations and the words in the *Thēsaurus Verbōrum*. Follow the model.

Abbreviations

nom.	nominative
gen.	genitive
dat.	dative
acc.	accusative
abl.	ablative
sing.	singular
pl.	plural

Thēsaurus Verbōrum

puella, -ae f.	girl
vir, virī m.	man
fīlius, -iī m.	son
vīnum, -ī n.	wine

→ virī   *gen. sing. nom. pl.*

1. virō _____ _____, _____ _____

2. puellīs _____ _____, _____ _____

3. fīliī _____ _____, _____ _____

4. puellā _____ _____

5. vīnum _____ _____, _____ _____

6. vīna _____ _____, _____ _____

10-13 Case Usage Review. Indicate which Latin case is used for each type of expression. Use only one case per expression, but a case can be used more than once. Use the abbreviations provided. Follow the model.

Abbreviations

nom.	nominative
gen.	genitive
dat.	dative
acc.	accusative
abl.	ablative
voc.	vocative

Case	Usage
→ nom.	Subject of the main verb
1. _____	Cost
2. _____	Direct object
3. _____	With adjectives like *idōneus* (suitable for)
4. _____	Time when
5. _____	BWIOF
6. _____	Object of a preposition showing motion toward
7. _____	Object of a compound verb
8. _____	Direct address
9. _____	Object of a preposition showing location
10. _____	Duration of time
11. _____	Indirect object
12. _____	Object of a preposition showing motion out of or away from

10-14 *Verba Discenda.* Select an English word that is a meaning for the Latin word. Some meanings given are not directly taken from the *Verba Discenda* list but rather represent synonyms of those meanings.

1. *cōgitō* (1) _____
2. *constō, constāre, constitī, constātum* _____
3. *super* (+ acc.) _____
4. *timeō, timēre, timuī* _____
5. *figūra, -ae* f. _____
6. *hīc* _____
7. *inspiciō, -ere, -exī, -ectum* _____
8. *praestō, praestāre, praestitī, praestātum* _____
9. *prōcēdō, prōcēdere, prōcessī, prōcessum* _____
10. *quam* _____
11. *antīquus, -a, -um* _____
12. *quantus, -a, -um* _____
13. *quattuor* _____
14. *parvus, -a, -um* _____
15. *ōvum, -ī* _____
16. *quinque* _____
17. *rogō* (1) _____
18. *sex* _____
19. *spectō* (1) _____

a. very old
b. cost
c. egg
d. exceed
e. four
f. go forward
g. be terrified
h. look over carefully
i. minuscule
j. on top of
k. ponder
l. how much
m. five
n. request
o. right here
p. six
q. shape
r. than
s. watch

10-15 Quantī Id Constat? Write five questions asking how much something costs. Remember that the cost of something is expressed in the ablative case. Then answer each question with an approropriate price. Don't worry about realistic prices. Use the *Verba Ūtenda* as a guide, and follow the model for your answers. You don't have to translate your sentences.

> ### VERBA ŪTENDA
>
> | **Merchandise** | **Numbers** | **Coins (all ablative)** |
> |---|---|---|
> | *ōvum, -ī* n. | *ūnus, -a, -um* | *asse, assibus* |
> | *cibus, -ī* m. | *duo, duae, duo* | *sestertiō, sestertiīs* |
> | *sīmia, -ae* m./f. | *trēs, tria* | *aureō, aureīs* |
> | *insula, -ae* f. | *quattuor* | *dēnāriō, dēnāriīs* |
> | *domus, -ī* f. | *quinque* | |
> | | *sex* | |

→ *Quantī ūnus sīmia constat?*   How much does one monkey cost?
Ūnus sīmia duōbus assibus constat.   One monkey costs two asses.

→ *Quantī duo sīmiae constant?*   How much do two monkeys cost?
Duo sīmiae tribus assibus constant. Two monkeys cost three asses.

How much?

1. _____
3. _____
5. _____
7. _____
9. _____

It costs . . .

2. _____
4. _____
6. _____
8. _____
10. _____

Name: _____   Date: _____

10-16 How Closely Did You Read? Use the *Thēsaurus Verbōrum* to indicate what is being described below.

Thēsaurus Verbōrum

Neuter
Capitoline Hill
Chaldaea

Pecūnia nōn olet
Templum Iūnōnis Monētae
Vespasian

1. Coins were minted here ____
2. The money does not stink ____
3. Neither male nor female ____

4. Jupiter's main temple stood here ____
5. Homeland of the astrologer ____
6. He taxed the urinals ____

10-17 Crossword Puzzle. Complete the puzzle using information from the chapter.

Across

1 – "To/for the slave girls"
3 – "To surpass"
6 – "Than"
8 – ____ of cost
9 – "Six"
10 – *Quattuor*
11 – ____ of price
13 – "Over"
14 – Temple of Jupiter on the Arx
17 – The nominative and ____ of all neuters look alike
19 – "Suitable," often used with dative

Down

2 – Latin name for country of astrologers and magicians
3 – All neuter nominative ____ end in -*a*
4 – "Old, ancient"
5 – The case of the indirect object
6 – "Five"
7 – "To/for Servilia"
10 – "Shape" in the dative singular
12 – ____ *id constat?* = How much does it cost?
15 – "I was afraid"
16 – "To/for the slaves"
17 – "To/for Aelius"
18 – The temple of Juno ____ was near the mint in Rome

11 Domum

11-01 Comprehension: *Lectiō Prīma*, **Latin Response.** Quote the Latin words from *Lectiō Prīma* that answer each question. The questions follow the order of the story. Follow the model.

→ Why are Licinia and Valeria happy?
propter verba bona astrologī

1. Why is Flavia tired? _____

2. Why is Socrates happy? _____

3. What is Aelius doing as the women approach their home? _____

4. What happens suddenly in line 9? _____

5. How does Socrates fight back? _____

6. What is Aelius holding in his hand? (lines 11–12) _____

7. What do the thieves look at tha scares them? _____

8. How is life in Rome described? (lines 16–17) _____

11-02 Comprehension *Lectiō Prīma: Quis est?* Select the noun that identifies who did something, based on *Lectiō Prīma*. There is only one correct answer for each question. Remember: *latro, latrōnis* m. thief, robber. Follow the model.

→ Quis holera et ōva ēmit?
   a. fēminae   **b.** Flāvia   **c.** Servīlius   **d.** Valeria

1. Quis dēlūbrō Iūnōnis Lūcīnae appropinquāvit?
   a. Aelius   **b.** astrologus   **c.** Valeria   **d.** latrōnēs

2. Quis oleum super aquam effūdit?
   a. Aelius   **b.** astrologus   **c.** fēminae   **d.** Flāvia

3. Quis laeta fuit quod nunc insula nōn longinqua fuit?
   a. Aelius   **b.** Flāvia   **c.** Sōcratēs   **d.** latrōnēs

4. Quis laetus fuit quod iēiūnus fuit et cibus domī fuit?
   a. Aelius   **b.** fēminae   **c.** Flāvia   **d.** Sōcratēs

5. Quis prō fabricā suā stetit et labōrāvit?
   a. Aelius   **b.** astrologus   **c.** Flāvia   **d.** Valeria

6. Quis ex angiportō subitō saluit?
   a. Aelius   **b.** latrō   **c.** fēminae   **d.** Sōcratēs

7. Quis ūnum latrōnem momordit?
   a. Aelius   **b.** Flāvia   **c.** latrōnēs   **d.** Sōcratēs

8. Quis celeriter sine saccō fugit?
   a. Aelius   **b.** astrologus   **c.** latrō   **d.** Sōcratēs

11-03 Infinitive Facts. Select the answer that best completes the sentence.

1. The infinitive is the _____ principal part of the verb.
   a. 1st   **b.** 2nd   **c.** 3rd   **d.** 4th

2. The best way to translate an infinitive is to use the word _____.
   a. having   **b.** for   **c.** to   **d.** was

3. An infinitive is a verbal _____.
   a. adjective   **b.** noun   **c.** adverb

4. In the English sentence "To dive without a partner is dangerous," the infinitive "to dive" is an example of what kind of infinitive in Latin?
   a. subjective infinitive   **b.** complementary infinitive   **c.** objective infinitive

5. In the English sentence "I love to ski," the infinitive "to ski" is an example of what kind of infinitive in Latin?
   a. subjective infinitive   **b.** complementary infinitive   **c.** objective infinitive

6. In the English sentence "I am unable to do that," the infinitive "to do" is an example of what kind of infinitive in Latin?
   a. subjective infinitive   **b.** complementary infinitive   **c.** objective infinitive

7. Latin infinitives have a gender. What is it?
   a. masculine   **b.** feminine   **c.** neuter

8. The subject of an infinitive goes in what case?
   a. nominative   **b.** dative   **c.** accusative   **d.** ablative

11-04 Phrases Controlling Infinitives. Indicate which type of infinitive each of the following Latin words/phrases introduces.

1. *volō:*
   a. complementary   **b.** objective   **c.** subjective

2. *iubeō:*
   a. complementary   **b.** objective   **c.** subjective

3. *malum est:*
   a. complementary   **b.** objective   **c.** subjective

4. *nōlō:*
   a. complementary   **b.** objective   **c.** subjective

5. *cupiō:*
   a. complementary   **b.** objective   **c.** subjective

6. *possum:*
   a. complementary   **b.** objective   **c.** subjective

7. *bonum est:*
   a. complementary   **b.** objective   **c.** subjective

8. *doceō:*
   a. complementary   **b.** objective   **c.** subjective

9. *mālō:*
   a. complementary   **b.** objective   **c.** subjective

10. *dēbeō:*
   a. complementary   **b.** objective   **c.** subjective

11-05 Choose the Correct Infinitive. Select the infinitive that best completes the sentence. Pay careful attention to the endings.

1. Lūcius [scrībere/scrībāre] nōn vult.
2. Tē [sedīre/sedēre] iubeō.
3. Amīcōs multōs [habere/habēre] bonum est.
4. Nōlō [abere/abīre].
5. Tē Latīnam linguam [dīcere/dīcēre] cupiō.
6. Nōn possum [dormere/dormīre].
7. Tē [currāre/currere] doceō.
8. Volō verba astrologī [audīre/audēre].

11-06 Comprehension. Use *Lectiō Secunda* to respond in Latin to the questions. Follow the model.

→ Who is Albus? Why is this name a joke?
   Canis est. Canis niger nōn albus est.

1. Where is everyone going in line 1? _____
2. How do they arrive at the house? _____
3. What has Caecilia Metella not heard about? _____
4. Who is asleep and what does Chiron do about it? _____
5. What did Lucius see? (lines 17–18) _____
6. Who owns the monkey? (lines 21–22) _____

11-07 Forming the Perfect Tense: All Persons. Use the perfect stem of the verb and the given subject to create the correct perfect tense form by adding the appropriate endings to the stem. Follow the models.

Perfect Stem	Subject	Form
→ advēn-	vōs	*advēnistis*
→ audīv-	ego et tū	*audīvimus*
1. festināv-	Marcus Lūciusque	_____
2. stet-	paedagōgus	_____
3. vīd-	ego et Lūcius	_____
4. audīv-	vir	_____
5. vīd-	vōs omnēs	_____
6. clamāv-	sīmia	_____
7. cucurr-	tū et ego	_____
8. fu-	nōs et tū	_____
9. potu-	Valeria Flāviaque	_____
10. mālu-	ego	_____

11-08 Present or Perfect? Select the correct tense for the verb in each sentence. Keep in mind the stem being used and then ask yourself if the endings are present or perfect.

1. Marcus ad Forum venit.   [present / perfect]
2. Marcus ad Forum vēnit.   [present / perfect]
3. Omnēs sīmiam audīvērunt.   [present / perfect]
4. Omnēs sīmiam audiunt.   [present / perfect]
5. Ego et sīmia per Forum currimus. [present / perfect]
6. Ego et sīmia per Forum cucurrimus. [present / perfect]
7. Flāvia ficōs vīdit.   [present / perfect]
8. Flāvia ficōs videt.   [present / perfect]

11-09 Sorting Verbs by Tense: Perfect. Select all the perfect tense verbs in the list.

_____ adveniunt   _____ dīcimus
_____ audīmus   _____ fuit
_____ audit   _____ dormītis
_____ audīvī   _____ es
_____ audīvistis   _____ sumus
_____ clāmāvistī   _____ surgimus
_____ clāmāvit   _____ surrexī
_____ cucurrit   _____ tollit
_____ curris   _____ vīdimus
_____ curritis   _____ voluit

11-10 Sorting Verbs by Number. Select all the plural verbs in the list, no matter the tense.

_____ adveniunt   _____ clāmāvit
_____ audīmus   _____ cucurrit
_____ audit   _____ curris
_____ audīvī   _____ curritis
_____ audīvistis   _____ dīcimus
_____ clāmāvistī   _____ fuit
_____ dormītis   _____ surrexī
_____ es   _____ tollit
_____ sumus   _____ vīdimus
_____ surgimus   _____ voluit

11-11 Sorting Verbs by Person: 1st Person. Select all the 1st person verbs in the list, both singular and plural, no matter the tense.

_____ adveniunt		_____ dīcimus
_____ audīmus		_____ fuit
_____ audit		_____ dormītis
_____ audīvī		_____ es
_____ audīvistis		_____ sumus
_____ clāmāvistī		_____ surgimus
_____ clāmāvit		_____ surrexī
_____ cucurrit		_____ tollit
_____ curris		_____ vīdimus
_____ curritis		_____ voluit

11-12 Sorting Verbs by Person: 2nd Person. Select all the 2nd person verbs in the list, both singular and plural, no matter the tense.

_____ adveniunt		_____ dīcimus
_____ audīmus		_____ fuit
_____ audit		_____ dormītis
_____ audīvī		_____ es
_____ audīvistis		_____ sumus
_____ clāmāvistī		_____ surgimus
_____ clāmāvit		_____ surrexī
_____ cucurrit		_____ tollit
_____ curris		_____ vīdimus
_____ curritis		_____ voluit

11-13 Sorting Verbs by Tense: Present. Select each present tense verb. Be sure to check the principal parts in the *Verba Omnia* at the back of the textbook to help you with stems.

_____ accidunt		_____ es
_____ adveniunt		_____ fuit
_____ audīmus		_____ nōvistī
_____ audit		_____ potuērunt
_____ audīvī		_____ salūtāvērunt
_____ audīvistis		_____ sumus
_____ clāmāvistī		_____ surgimus
_____ clāmāvit		_____ surrexī
_____ cucurrit		_____ tollit
_____ curris		_____ vīdērunt
_____ curritis		_____ vīdimus
_____ dīcit		_____ voluit
_____ dīxī		_____ vult
_____ dormītis		

11-14 Remembering Caesar. Use the *Thēsaurus Verbōrum* to complete these famous sayings by Julius Caesar. Not every answer is used.

Thēsaurus Verbōrum

casta	magnī	trēs
duo	nōlunt	tū
iacta	omnis	volunt
in	parvīs	vōs

1. Ālea _____ est.

2. Et _____, Brūte?

3. Gallia est _____ dīvīsa in partēs **4.** _____.

11-15 *Verba Discenda.* Match the English to the Latin *Verbum Discendum.*

1. *adveniō, advenīre, advēnī, adventum* _____   **a.** goddess

2. *appropinquō* (1) _____   **b.** approach

3. *cūr* _____   **c.** bag

4. *dea, -ae* f. _____   **d.** come to

5. *ecce* _____   **e.** far off

6. *fortasse* _____   **f.** get to know

7. *longē* _____   **g.** jump

8. *noscō, noscere, nōvī, nōtum* _____   **h.** Look!

9. *saccus, -ī* m. _____   **i.** maybe

10. *saliō, salīre, saliī/saluī, saltum* _____   **j.** raise

11. *sīc* _____   **k.** so

12. *subitō* _____   **l.** suddenly

13. *tam* _____   **m.** very

14. *tollō, tollere, sustulī, sublātum* _____   **n.** why

15. *valdē* _____   **o.** word

16. *verbum, -ī* n. _____   **p.** yes

11-16 How Carefully Did You Read? Complete each sentence with the correct word from the *Thēsaurus Verbōrum.* Not all the words in the *Thēsaurus* are used.

Thēsaurus Verbōrum

complementary	neuter
feminine	objective
infinitive	subjective
masculine	supplementary

1. A(n) _____ is a verbal noun.

2. _____ infinitives are used to complete the action of certain verbs, like *volō, nōlō, mālō, possum,* and *dēbeō.*

3. _____ infinitives are used as the direct object of certain verbs, like *cupiō* (I wish), *doceō* (I teach), *vetō* (I forbid), and *iubeō* (I order).

4. _____ infinitives are commonly accompanied by a form of *est.*

5. The gender of all Latin infinitives is _____.

11-17 Crossword Puzzle. Complete the puzzle with information from the chapter.

Across

2 – The gender of infinitives

6 – "I am unable to dance." What kind of infinitive?

8 – "Far away"

9 – "Suddenly"

10 – "Word"

12 – "I love to dance." What kind of infinitive?

13 – Subject of an infinitive goes in this case

16 – "To have come"

17 – *Vēnī, vīdī, _____*

18 – "You (sing.) came"

Down

1 – "They came"

3 – "To leap"

4 – "Very"

5 – "Y'all came"

6 – A famous governor of Gaul

7 – "Lutetia"

9 – "To dance is pure joy." What kind of infinitive?

11 – "Goddess"

14 – *Et _____, Brūte?*

15 – "He came"

16 – "We came"

19 – "Thus"

20 – *Ālea _____ est.*

12 In Domō Magnā

12-01 Verbs with the Dative: Substitution Practice. For each sentence substitute the dative of the form in parentheses for the original dative (in **bold**). Keep the number the same. Rewrite the entire sentence with the new word.

→ **Tibi** nōn crēdō.
(Marcus) *Marcō nōn crēdō.*

1. Nōn **Valeriae** placet.
   (fīlius) _____
   (paedagōgus) _____
   (sīmia) _____
   (Aelius) _____

2. Pater **Servīliae** respondet.
   (Lūcius)_____
   (Marcus) _____
   (servus) _____
   (ancilla) _____

3. Servīlius **servīs** imperat.
   (ancillae) _____
   (puerī) _____
   (puellae) _____
   (fēminae) _____

4. Nōs **linguae Latīnae** studēmus.
   (rhētorica) _____
   (Forum Rōmānum) _____
   (Rōma) _____
   (vīta Rōmāna) _____

12-02 Special Verbs That Take the Dative: Vocabulary. Match the English definition to the Latin verb.

1. *crēdō* _____
2. *ignoscō* _____
3. *imperō* _____
4. *noceō* _____
5. *parcō* _____
6. *persuādeō* _____
7. *placeō* _____
8. *studeō* _____

a. be eager to/for
b. be pleasing to
c. command
d. forgive
e. harm
f. persuade
g. spare
h. trust

12-03 Verb Transformation. Read *Lectiō Prīma* before doing this exercise. Have the characters themselves answer the following questions. This sometimes involves changing the person in the original sentence. Use *ita* for a "yes" answer and *nōn* for a negative. Follow the model.

→ Ō paedagōge, fuistīne valdē īrātus?
Ita, īrātus fuī.

1. Ō paedagōge et sīmia, cucurristisne strēnuē?

_____

2. Ō paedagōge, cēpitne sīmia saccum furtīvē?

_____

3. Ō paedagōge et sīmia, cucurristisne tōtum per Forum longē?

_____

4. Ō paedagōge, potuistīne sīmiam in Forō capere?

_____

5. Ō paedagōge, territusne fuistī?

_____

6. Ō paedagōge, amīsistīne pecūniam Servīliī?

_____

12-04 Translating Special Verbs More Than One Way. Retranslate each sentence to include the word "to" or "for." Follow the model.

→ *Sīmiae parcit.*   He spares the monkey.
                            He shows mercy to the monkey.

1. *Lūdus Lūciō nōn placet.*   School does not please Lucius. _____
2. *Virīs crēdō.*   I believe the men. _____
3. *Paedagōgus sīmiae ignōvit.*   The paedagogus pardoned the monkey. _____
4. *Ancillae imperāvimus.*   We commanded the maid servant. _____
5. *Num puellīs nocēmus?*   We are not harming the girls, are we? _____
6. *Puer magistrīs respondit.*   The boy answered the teachers. _____

12-05 Translating Datives with Special Verbs. Translate these sentences into idiomatic English, paying attention to the special verbs.

1. Placetne lūdus tibi?

_____

2. Crēditisne magistrō?

_____

3. Magistrī puerīs malīs nōn ignōvērunt.

_____

4. Amīcī amīcīs imperant.

_____

5. Nōnne tibi nocent?

_____

6. Discipulī magistrō respondērunt.

_____

12-06 Impersonal Verbs: Accusative or Dative? Select the accusative or dative form of the word, depending on the rules for that particular impersonal verb.

1. [Discipulīs/Discipulōs] studēre necesse est.

2. [Mihi/Mē] abīre necesse est.

3. [Mihi/Mē] abīre oportet.

4. [Mihi/Mē] currere nōn placet.

5. [Virīs/Virōs] abīre nunc licet.

6. [Sīmiīs/Sīmīas] vīnum bibere nōn licet.

7. [Puerīs/Puerōs] in tabernā vīnum bibere nōn oportet.

8. [Paedagōgō/Paedagōgum] cum Lūciō ambulāre necesse est.

9. [Lūciō/Lūcium] in lūdō nōn male facere oportet.

10. [Magistrō/Magistrum] puerī nōn placent.

12-07 Making Adverbs. Make each of the following adjectives into adverbs. All you usually have to do is drop the ending and add -ē. Then translate the adverb into English. There are two slightly irregular adverbs here. Follow the model.

→ furtīvus   *furtīvē*   secretly

1. īrāta   _____   _____

2. longum   _____   _____

3. strēnuī   _____   _____

4. timidae   _____   _____

5. validōs   _____   _____

6. bonus   _____   _____

12-08 Adverbs in Context. Make the adverb from the adjective in parentheses. A few new words are given in the *Thēsaurus Verbōrum*.

Thēsaurus Verbōrum

cantō (1)   sing
coquō -ere   cook

→ Valeria _____ coquit. (bonus)
Valeria _____ bene _____ coquit.

1. Servīlia _____ cantat (laetus).
2. Chīrōn prō discipulīs _____ stat. (īrātus)
3. Latrōnēs _____ cucurrērunt. (furtīvus)
4. Fēminae in tabernā _____ labōrant. (strēnuus)
5. Flāvia Sōcratem _____ portat. (longus)
6. Lūcius _____ sedet sub virgā Chīrōnis. (timidus)

12-09 GNC'ing! Nominative Case. Indicate which adjective form GNCs with the noun in each sentence. Be sure you have read the *Angulus Grammaticus* about PAINS words.

1. Lūcius nōn _____ est.
   a. laetus   **b.** laetius   **c.** laeta   **d.** laetum

2. Puer nōn _____ est.
   a. laetus   **b.** laetius   **c.** laeta   **d.** laeter

3. Puella nōn _____ est.
   a. laetus   **b.** laetius   **c.** laeta   **d.** laetum

4. Nauta nōn _____ est.
   a. laetus   **b.** laetius   **c.** laeta   **d.** laetum

5. Agricolae nōn _____ sunt.
   a. laetus   **b.** laetī   **c.** laetae   **d.** laetum

6. Sex ōva _____ emere volō.
   a. bonum   **b.** bonus   **c.** bonae   **d.** bona

7. Virum _____ nōn videō.
   a. magnus   **b.** magnum   **c.** magnam

8. Vīnum _____ bibō.
   a. bonus   **b.** bonam   **c.** bonum

9. Nautae _____ ad tabernam ambulant.
   a. multae   **b.** multus   **c.** multa   **d.** multī

10. Virī _____ prō tabernā sunt.
   a. iēiūnus   **b.** iēiūnae   **c.** iēiūnī   **d.** iēiūna

12-10 GNC'ing! All Cases. Select the word that provides the proper GNC for the word in bold. Be sure you have read the *Angulus Grammaticus* about PAINS words.

1. **Caecilia** Servīliī uxor _____ est.
   a. secundus   b. secunda   c. secundī   d. secundum

2. Chīrōn nōn **vir** _____ est.
   a. malus   b. mala   c. malum   d. maler

3. Nōmen **paedagōgī** _____ nōn Chīrōn est.
   a. malus   b. malī   c. malae   d. malum

4. Valeria **poētae** _____ pōtum dat.
   a. bonae   b. bonī   c. bonō   d. bonīs

5. Vidētisne **nautās** _____?
   a. bonās   b. bonīs   c. bonōs   d. bonī

6. _____ **incolae** Rōmae multam pecūniam habent.
   a. Paucae   b. Paucī   c. Pauca   d. Paucō

7. Valeria cibum **virīs** _____ dat.
   a. multīs   b. multōs   c. multae   d. multō

8. Nōmen **ancillae** _____ Flāvia est.
   a. Germānica   b. Germānicam   c. Germānicae   d. Germānicīs

9. Servīlius dominus **servōrum** _____ est.
   a. multī   b. multus   c. multae   d. multōrum

10. Rōma **incōlās** _____ habet.
    a. multī   b. multam   c. multōs   d. multum

12-11 GNC'ing! Switching Number. Select the choice that is the other number for the noun/adjective pair in **bold**. If it is singular select the pair that is plural, and if plural select the singular. Keep the case and gender the same. Follow the model.

→ **Fīlia** Valeriae **bona** est.
   a. filiam bonam   b. filiās bonās   c. *filiae bonae*

1. **Magistrī bonī** bene docent.
   a. Magister boner   b. Magister bona   c. Magister bonus

2. Paucī Rōmānī **lectīcās ornātās** habent.
   a. lectīcae ornātae   b. lectīcam ornātam   c. lectīca ornāta

3. **Fīliī fessī** nōn labōrant.
   a. Fīlius fessus   b. Fīlium fessum   c. Fīliō fessō

4. Fēmina **poētae parvō** pōtum dat.
   a. poētās parvōs   b. poētae parvī   c. poētīs parvīs

5. **Poētae malī** carmina (*poems*) mihi nōn placent.
   a. Poētīs malīs   b. Poētam malam   c. Poētārum malōrum

6. Vidētisne **nautās malōs**?
   a. nautam malam   b. nautam malum   c. nautae malae

12-12 Vocabulary of a Roman House. Match each Latin word with its description.

1. *ālae* ____
2. *ātrium* ____
3. *compluvium* ____
4. *cubiculum* ____
5. *culīna* ____
6. *faucēs* ____
7. *iānitor* ____
8. *impluvium* ____
9. *peristȳlium* ____
10. *tablīnum* ____
11. *trīclīnium* ____
12. *vestibulum* ____

a. a slave who guarded the door and controlled access to the home
b. entryway into a Roman house; originally a place to hang one's cloak
c. Latin word for "jaws" or another word for the *vestibulum*
d. the main public room of the house where guests were greeted
e. a pool in the center of the *ātrium*
f. an opening in the roof over the *ātrium*
g. the "wings" or rooms on either side of the *ātrium*
h. bedroom
i. office where the head of the house conducted business
j. a colonnaded garden toward the back of the house
k. dining room
l. kitchen

12-13 How Closely Did You Read? The four grammatical concepts discussed in Chapter 12 are:

a. Adverbs
b. Datives with special verbs
c. GNC'ing
d. Impersonal verbs

One of these concepts appears in each of the following words or phrases. Use the letters provided to indicate which grammatical concept is illustrated by each word or phrase. Follow the model.

→ __*c*__ avus aeger

____ 1. Cibō studēmus
____ 2. domus magna
____ 3. furtīvē
____ 4. Sīmiae parcō.
____ 5. Magistrī discipulīs placent.
____ 6. Mihi respondēte!
____ 7. Nōn sīmiīs pecūniam habēre licet!
____ 8. Mihi sīmiam capere necesse est!
____ 9. īrātē
____ 10. uxor secunda

12-14 *Verba Discenda.* Select the correct English translation for each Latin word.

1. *annus, -ī* m. _____   **a.** bedroom
2. *cēna, -ae* f. _____   **b.** conquer
3. *cēnō* (1) _____   **c.** dine
4. *cubiculum, -ī* n. _____   **d.** dinner
5. *decem* _____   **e.** fight
6. *dormiō* _____   **f.** do injury to
7. *duodecim* _____   **g.** it is necessary to
8. *fugiō* _____   **h.** live
9. *habitō* _____ (1)   **i.** one ought
10. *necesse est* _____   **j.** please (verb)
11. *noceō* _____   **k.** make ready
12. *oportet* _____   **l.** run away
13. *parcō* _____   **m.** show mercy to
14. *parō* _____   **n.** sleep
15. *placeō* _____   **o.** ten
16. *pugnō* _____   **p.** to devote oneself to
17. *studeō* _____   **q.** twelve
18. *vīgintī* _____   **r.** twenty
19. *vincō* _____   **s.** year

12-15 *Verba Discenda.* Use your knowledge of this chapter's *Verba Discenda* to help you select the correct definition of each English word. The key part of each word is in bold.

1. im**pugn** _____
2. per**enn**ial _____
3. **decim**ation _____
4. in**noce**nt _____
5. **victor**ious _____
6. **dorm**ition _____
7. **dorm**ant _____
8. **fug**ue state _____
9. **cena**culum _____
10. **nox**ious _____

a. A psychiatric disorder in which the person's memory disappears and then reappears

b. A punitive custom of Roman generals in which every tenth soldier was killed; devastation

c. A room in Jerusalem believed to be the site of the Last Supper

d. Doing no harm

e. Eastern Orthodox feast day celebrating the day on which Mary fell asleep and went to heaven

f. Having won

g. Inactive, as if asleep

h. Injurious to health

i. Lasting an entire year or more

j. To challenge, assail

12-16 Crossword Puzzle. Complete the puzzle with information from the chapter.

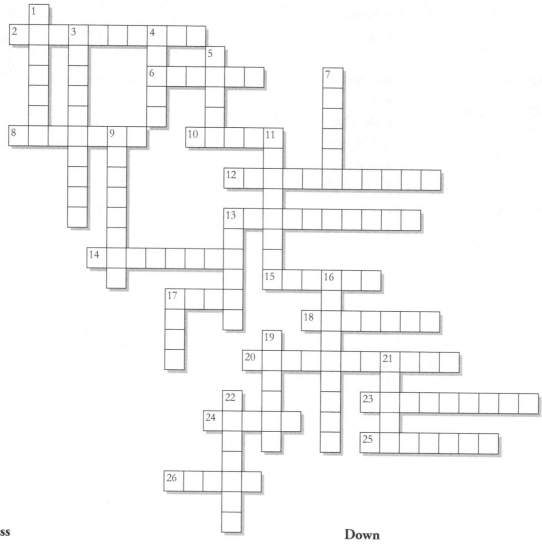

Across

2 – Passageway from front door in a Roman house

6 – Kitchen in a Roman house

8 – "20"

10 – The P in PAINS

12 – Colonnaded garden area in a Roman house

13 – "It is necessary to"

14 – "12"

15 – First main room one saw coming into a Roman house

17 – The C in GNC

18 – "One ought"

20 – City destroyed along with Pompeii

23 – Bedroom in a Roman house

24 – "I harm"

25 – Slave who guarded the door

26 – "I flee"

Down

1 – *Parcō*, 3rd principal part

3 – Dining room in a Roman house

4 – "It is permitted"

5 – "I conquer"

7 – "It is pleasing"

9 – The master's office in a Roman house

11 – The A in PAINS

13 – The N in GNC

16 – Rain water cistern in the *ātrium*

17 – "Dinner"

19 – The G in GNC

21 – The N in PAINS

22 – "I have slept"

13 Māter et Fīlia

13-01 Declining the 3rd Declension. Supply the missing forms in the following chart for the 3rd declension nouns *frāter* and *nōmen*. Pay attention to the different endings for neuter nouns.

	3rd Declension	
Case	**Masculine/Feminine**	**Neuter**
	Singular	
Nominative	frāter	nōmen
Genitive	frātris	nōminis
Dative	1. _____	9. _____
Accusative	frātrem	10. _____
Ablative	2. _____	11. _____
Vocative	3. _____	12. _____
	Plural	
Nominative	frātrēs	nōmina
Genitive	4. _____	13. _____
Dative	5. _____	14. _____
Accusative	6. _____	15. _____
Ablative	7. _____	nōminibus
Vocative	8. _____	16. _____

13-02 Identifying Noun Stems. Use the grammatical information provided to identify the stems of the following 3rd declension nouns.

1. *homō, hominis* m./f. _____
2. *frāter, frātris* m. _____
3. *nōmen, nōminis* n. _____
4. *opus, operis* n. _____
5. *tempus, temporis* n. _____
6. *pater, patris* m. _____
7. *nēmō, nēminis* m./f. _____
8. *vox, vōcis* f. _____
9. *soror, sorōris* f. _____
10. *senātor, senātōris* m. _____

13-03 Identifying 3rd Declension Forms. Now identify the case and number of each 3rd declension noun marked in **bold**. Follow the model.

	Case	Number
➔ **Tonsōrī** pecūniam dō.	dative	singular
1. Multī **actōrēs** in Forō sunt.	_____	_____
2. Ambulat cum **latrōnibus.**	_____	_____
3. Tabernae **fullōnum** prope Forum sunt.	_____	_____
4. Haec **holera** vendere volō.	_____	_____
5. Nōmen **mātris** Caecilia est.	_____	_____
6. Hominēs audiō.	_____	_____
7. Fīliae **mātribus** suīs placent.	_____	_____
8. Sīmia ā **frātre** meō currit.	_____	_____

13-04 Declining the 3rd Declension. Select one 3rd declension masculine or feminine noun and one 3rd declension neuter noun from the list, and decline each one.

homō, hominis m./f. human being, person, man
māter, mātris f. mother
ōs, ōris n. mouth, face
pater, patris m. father
soror, sorōris f. sister
tempus, tempōris n. time, season

Case	Masculine/Feminine	Neuter
	Singular	
Nominative	1. _____	13. _____
Genitive	2. _____	14. _____
Dative	3. _____	15. _____
Accusative	4. _____	16. _____
Ablative	5. _____	17. _____
Vocative	6. _____	18. _____
	Plural	
Nominative	7. _____	19. _____
Genitive	8. _____	20. _____
Dative	9. _____	21. _____
Accusative	10. _____	22. _____
Ablative	11. _____	23. _____
Vocative	12. _____	24. _____

13-05 3rd Declension in Context. Select the 3rd declension noun that grammatically completes the sentence. Follow the model.

→ _____ vīdī.
   a. Hominī   **b.** *Frātrem*   **c.** Mātris

(Only *frātrem* can be the direct object of *vīdī*. The other nouns are not accusative.)

1. _____ currit.
   a. Nēminī   **b.** Frātrem   **c.** Māter

2. Servīlius _____ pecūniam multam dat.
   a. patre   **b.** hominibus   **c.** nēminem

3. Servī _____ vōcēs audiunt.
   a. senātōrum   **b.** sorōribus   **c.** hominēs

4. Senātōrēs _____ in Forō vīdērunt.
   a. hominēs   **b.** nēmō   **c.** frātre

5. _____ nōn habeō.
   a. Nōminum   **b.** Nōmen   **c.** Māter

6. Multī _____ in Forō sunt.
   a. mātrēs   **b.** patrum   **c.** patrēs

7. Sciō (*I know*) nōmina _____.
   a. frātribus   **b.** hominī   **c.** patrum

8. _____ dē Augustō mala verba dīcit.
   a. Hominēs   **b.** Frātre   **c.** Nēmō

13-06 False Friend Endings: 1st and 3rd Declensions. Select the endings that are common to both the 1st and 3rd declensions. These can sometimes lead you astray and are called "false friends" as a result. Don't forget the vocative case.

_____ -em	_____ -ae	_____ -ās
_____ -am	_____ -īs	_____ -e
_____ -um	_____ -is	_____ -ēs
_____ -ibus	_____ -ī	_____ -a
_____ -ārum	_____ -ō	_____ -ā

13-07 False Friend Endings: 2nd and 3rd Declensions. Select the endings that are common to both the 2nd and 3rd declensions. These can sometimes lead you astray and are called "false friends" as a result. Don't forget the vocative case.

_____ -em	_____ -ae	_____ -e
_____ -am	_____ -īs	_____ -ēs
_____ -um	_____ -ī	_____ -a
_____ -ibus	_____ -ō	_____ -ā
_____ -ārum	_____ -ās	

13-08 False Friend Endings: All Three Declensions.
Some endings mean one thing in one declension and something else in another declension. Identify and select the right choice for each ending in the declension indicated. Follow the model.

→ -um (3rd)
  a. accusative singular   **b.** *genitive plural*

1. -e (2nd)
  a. nominative plural   **b.** vocative singular

2. -ī (2nd)
  a. dative singular   **b.** nominative plural

3. -a (1st)
  a. nominative singular   **b.** neuter nominative plural

4. -a (3rd)
  a. nominative singular   **b.** neuter nominative plural

5. -ī (3rd)
  a. dative singular   **b.** nominative plural

6. -um (3rd)
  a. genitive plural   **b.** accusative singular

7. -um (2nd)
  a. genitive plural   **b.** masculine/neuter accusative sing.

8. -um (2nd)
  a. genitive plural   **b.** neuter nominative sing.

13-09 Possibilities.
As you read Latin you must always know what declension a word belongs to so that "false friends" don't lead you astray! Decide which of the two choices is a possible number and case for the given word considering its declension and gender. Follow the model.

→ nōminī [nom. pl./dat. sing.] *dat. sing.* (The ending -*ī* can be nom. pl. but only on a 2nd declension word. This is a 3rd declension word.)

1. ancillīs [abl. pl./gen. sing.]
2. frātris [dat. pl./gen. sing.]
3. hominēs [nom. pl./abl. pl.]
4. hominī [nom. pl./dat. sing.]
5. hominum [acc. sing./gen. pl.]
6. mātrem [acc. sing./gen. pl.]
7. nōmina [nom. sing./acc. pl.]
8. mātribus [dat. pl./nom. sing.]
9. servī [dat. sing./gen. sing.]
10. servum [acc. sing./gen. pl.]
11. serve [voc. sing./abl. sing.]
12. ancillae [abl. sing./dat. sing.]

13-10 GNC'ing! 2-1-2 Adjectives with 3ʳᵈ Declension Nouns. Indicate which adjective form GNC's with the noun in each sentence. Follow the model.

→ Soror Lūciī_____ est.

a. pulchor   **b.** pulchrae   **c.** pulcher   **d.** *pulchra*

(The adjective *pulcher, -chra, -chrum* is a 2-1-2 adjective and must use endings from those declensions, attached to its stem.)

1. Māter nōn _____ est.

a. laetus   **b.** laetius   **c.** laeta   **d.** laeter

2. Mātrēs nōn _____ sunt.

a. laetī   **b.** laetae   **c.** laetēs   **d.** laeter

3. Pater nōn _____ est.

a. laetus   **b.** laetius   **c.** laeta   **d.** laeter

4. Patrēs nōn _____ sunt.

a. laetī   **b.** laetēs   **c.** laeter   **d.** laetum

5. Nōmen _____ habeō.

a. bonus   **b.** bonam   **c.** bonium   **d.** bonum

6. Nōmina _____ habēmus.

a. bonus   **b.** bona   **c.** bonum   **d.** bonam

7. Patrem _____ habeō.

a. bonus   **b.** bonam   **c.** bonium   **d.** bonum

8. Mātrēs _____ habēmus.

a. bonus   **b.** bonam   **c.** bonās   **d.** bonēs

9. Patrēs _____ habēmus.

a. bonōs   **b.** bonam   **c.** bonās   **d.** bonēs

10. Frātrī _____ pecūniam paedagōgus dat.

a. meum   **b.** meī   **c.** meam   **d.** meō

13-11 GNC'ing 3ʳᵈ Declension Nouns. Complete each sentence with the form of *suus, -a, -um* that agrees with the word marked in **bold**. Indicate in parentheses how *suus* is translated here.

→ Servīlius **uxōrem** _____ amat. (_____)

   *Servīlius uxōrem **suam** amat.* (his)

1. Flāvia cum **dominā** _____ ambulat. (_____)

2. Licinia **mātris** _____ pecūniam nōn habet. (_____)

3. Lūcius **sorōrī** _____ passerem nōn dat. (_____)

4. Lūcius **sorōrem** _____ nōn vocat. (_____)

5. Puerī vōcēs **mātrum** _____ audiunt. (_____)

6. Puerī **mātrēs** _____ valdē amant. (_____)

7. Servīlia nōmen **patris** _____ dīcit. (_____)

8. Puerī cum **mātribus** _____ ambulant. (_____)

9. Servīlia **frātrī** _____ cibum dat. (_____)

10. Lūcius **frātrem** _____ videt. (_____)

13-12 Composition. Review your 3rd declension endings by selecting the Latin word that best translates the underlined word(s).

1. This is <u>mother's</u> favorite.
   - **a.** mātrēs
   - **b.** mātris
   - **c.** mātrum
   - **d.** mātrī

2. Give the candy <u>to father</u>.
   - **a.** patrī
   - **b.** patrem
   - **c.** patris
   - **d.** patribus

3. I know many <u>people</u>.
   - **a.** hominem
   - **b.** hominēs
   - **c.** hominum
   - **d.** homine

4. What is his <u>name</u>?
   - **a.** nōminis
   - **b.** nōmina
   - **c.** nōmen
   - **d.** nōminibus

5. <u>No one</u> is here.
   - **a.** nēminis
   - **b.** nēminem
   - **c.** nēmō
   - **d.** nēmine

6. I heard my master's <u>voice</u>.
   - **a.** vōcis
   - **b.** vox
   - **c.** vōcibus
   - **d.** vōcem

7. I gave the money to my <u>sisters</u>.
   - **a.** sorōris
   - **b.** sorōribus
   - **c.** sorōrēs
   - **d.** sorōrī

8. I went with the <u>senators</u> yesterday.
   - **a.** senātōrēs
   - **b.** senātōris
   - **c.** senātōribus
   - **d.** senātōrum

9. The <u>merchants'</u> shops are not far.
   - **a.** mercātor
   - **b.** mercātōris
   - **c.** mercātōribus
   - **d.** mercātōrum

10. The <u>barber's</u> shop is here.
   - **a.** tonsor
   - **b.** tonsōris
   - **c.** tonsōribus
   - **d.** tonsōrum

13-13 3rd Declension in Context. Select the form of the 3rd declension noun that makes the best grammatical sense for the sentence.

1. Puerī [mātre / mātris] in viā currunt.
2. Duo ōva [patrī / patre] dedī.
3. Suntne multī [hominēs / hominī] prope tabernam?
4. Paedagōgus cum [frātrem / frātre] meō ambulat.
5. Nōlī illud (*that*) in [ōribus / ōre] tuō pōnere.
6. Sunt quattuor [tempus / tempora] annī (*seasons of the year*).

13-14 Latīna Hodierna: Derivatives. Based on your new knowledge of Latin words for family relationships, match the meaning with its correct English word.

1. avuncular _____
2. filial _____
3. fraternity _____
4. matriarch _____
5. patriarch _____
6. sorority _____

   - **a.** pertaining to a son or a daughter
   - **b.** male head of a clan or family
   - **c.** female head of a clan or family
   - **d.** characteristic of an uncle
   - **e.** a band of women who consider themselves sisters
   - **f.** a band of men who consider themselves brothers

13-15 _Verba Discenda._ Select the English translation for each Latin word.

1. _amīca_ _____
2. _amō_ _____
3. _cārus_ _____
4. _cūrō_ _____
5. _frāter_ _____
6. _homō_ _____
7. _iēiūnus_ _____
8. _intellegō_ _____
9. _māter_ _____
10. _nēmō_ _____
11. _ōs_ _____
12. _pater_ _____
13. _pulcher_ _____
14. _quam_ _____
15. _soror_ _____
16. _taceō_ _____
17. _tempus_ _____
18. _vīta_ _____

a. be silent
b. brother
c. care for
d. expensive
e. father
f. girlfriend
g. handsome
h. how!
i. hungry
j. life
k. love
l. mother
m. mouth
n. nobody
o. person
p. season
q. sister
r. understand

13-16 _Verba Discenda_: Missing Parts. A dictionary entry has several parts to it, and they are all useful to know. You have to memorize these for _Verba Discenda_. Fill in the missing information for each word. Follow the models.

→ cārus, _-a, -um_   dear, expensive
→ taceō, tacēre, _tacuī,_   tacitum be quiet, be silent
→ frāter, frātris _m._   brother

1. _amīca,_ _____ f. friend, girlfriend
2. _homō,_ _____ m./f. person, human being, man
3. _intellegō, intellegere,_ _____, _intellectum_ understand
4. _nēmō,_ _____ m./f. nobody
5. _ōs, ōris_ _____ mouth, face
6. _pulcher,_ _____, _pulchrum_ pretty, handsome
7. _quam_ _____
8. _soror,_ _____ f. sister
9. _tempus, temporis_ _____ time, season
10. _vīta,_ _____ f. life

13-17 How Closely Did You Read? Match each word to its description.

1. A town subject to Rome but governed by its own laws ____

2. Catullus' home town ____

3. Catullus' lover ____

4. Copying someone else's work without citing it ____

5. Greek poetess, source for Catullus ____

6. Poet; contemporary of Caesar ____

7. Province just south of the Italian Alps ____

8. *Pater māterque filiīque servīque* ____

9. *Soror Lūciī Marcīque* ____

10. The Latin word for a married woman ____

a. Verona

b. Gallia Cisalpīna

c. Servīlia

d. *familia*

e. Lesbia

f. *mūnicipium*

g. Sappho

h. plagiarism

i. Catullus

j. *matrōna*

13-18 Crossword Puzzle. Complete the puzzle with information from the chapter.

Across

1 – 3rd principal part of *taceō*
3 – Favorite poet of Servilia
6 – I saw "the people" in the Forum
7 – "Life"
9 – "Uncle"
12 – The 3rd declension has nouns of this many genders
15 – Head of a Roman household
17 – Servilia's heartthrob
20 – *nēmō*, _____, m./f. nobody
21 – The "G" in GNC

Down

1 – "To be silent"
2 – The genitive singular ending for all 3rd declension nouns
4 – "Girlfriend"
5 – "Household"
6 – I gave a meal "to the man"
7 – Hometown of both Valeria and Catullus
8 – A relatively independent town
10 – "I care for"
11 – Famous Greek poetess
13 – *os*, _____, n. face
14 – "Expensive"
16 – "Hungry"
18 – He used Vergil in his Divine Comedy
19 – The "C" in GNC
20 – The "N" in GNC

14   Dē Perseō

14-01 Noun and Adjective Stems in -er. Select the correct stem of each -er word.

1. *ager, agrī* m.: [ager- / agr-]
2. *liber, librī* m.: [liber- / libr-]
3. *puer, puerī* m.: [puer- / pur-]
4. *pulcher, pulchra, pulchrum*: [pulcher- / pulchr-]
5. *līber, lībera, līberum* [līber- / lībr-]

14-02 GNC'ing! Nouns and Adjectives in -er. Select the correct adjective form for each noun.

1. ager:
   a. magnus   b. magna   c. magnum
2. puer:
   a. boner   b. bonus   c. bonum
3. liber:
   a. mea   b. meus   c. meum
4. puer:
   a. pulchra   b. pulchrus   c. pulcher
5. agrō:
   a. līberō   b. lībrō   c. liberō
6. homō:
   a. līber   b. lībrus   c. liberus
7. soror:
   a. pulchera   b. pulchra   c. pulcher
8. puerōrum:
   a. pulcherōrum   b. pulchrum   c. pulchrōrum
9. librum:
   a. magnus   b. magna   c. magnum
10. frāter
   a. pulcherus   b. pulcher   c. pulchrer

14-03 Deceptive Pairs. What do these phrases mean in English? **Hint:** Pay attention to the macrons and to *-(e)r-* in the stems in these very similar Latin words.

> *liber, librī* m. book (stem *libr-*)
>
> *līber, lībera, līberum* free (stem *līber-*)
>
> *līberī, -ōrum* m. pl. children (stem *līber-*)

If you pronounce them aloud, it is much simpler because of the long and short *-i* vowel.

1. puer līber
   a. the boy's book   **b.** the free boy

2. puerī līberī
   a. the boy's books   **b.** the boys' books   **c.** of the free boy

3. librī pulchrī
   a. the beautiful books   **b.** the beautiful free people

4. līberī pulchrī
   a. the beautiful books   **b.** the beautiful children

5. librī līberī
   a. the children's books   **b.** the free books   **c.** the child's books

6. līberī līberī
   a. the free children   **b.** the free books

14-04 Noun Adjective Pairs: 3ʳᵈ Declension. Identify the gender, number, and case of the following pairs. Be sure to follow the model closely.

	Gender	Number	Case
→ tempestātēs magnae	*feminine*	*plural*	*nominative*
1. tempestātēs magnās			
2. tempestātis magnae			
3. tempestātī magnae			
4. mātrem cāram			
5. actōribus novīs			
6. tranquillum mare			
7. hostem malum			
8. rēgum bonōrum			

14-05 Substantives. Choose the correct translation of the substantive in bold in the following sentences. Remember to translate a neuter as "thing/things," a feminine as "woman/women," and a masculine as "man/men."

1. Valeria **multa** videt.
   a. many women
   b. many things
   c. many men

2. **Paucī** dē theātrō dīcunt.
   a. a few men
   b. a few things
   c. a few women

3. **Paucae** dē theātrō dīcunt.
   a. a few men
   b. a few things
   c. a few women

4. Paedagōgus **pauca** dīcit.
   a. few women
   b. few things
   c. few men

5. Dē **bonīs** māter dīcit.
   a. a good thing
   b. a good woman
   c. good men

6. Marcus **pulchrās** vidēre vult.
   a. pretty women
   b. a pretty woman
   c. pretty things

7. **Bonī** bonum vīnum amant.
   a. good things
   b. good men
   c. of a good man

8. **Bona** filiōs amat!
   a. good things
   b. a good thing
   c. a good woman

14-06 Translating Substantives. Select the sentence that best translates the Latin substantives.

1. *Bonōs nōn mala dīcere oportet.*
   a. Bad people shouldn't say good things.
   b. Good people shouldn't say bad things.

2. *Bonī saepe mala cupiunt.*
   a. Good people often want bad things.
   b. Bad people often want good things.

3. *Malōs bonī semper vincunt.*
   a. Bad people always defeat good ones.
   b. Good people always defeat bad ones.

4. *Nōlīte dē malīs bona dīcere!*
   a. Good people shouldn't speak about bad people.
   b. Don't say good things about bad people.

14-07 Which Substantive? Select the Latin word that correctly represents the English word in bold. If you don't know the meaning of the word, it will be clear from context. Be sure to choose the right number and the case the word would be in Latin.

1. **Dead men** tell no tales. [Mortua / Mortuī]

2. I really like that movie, "The Good, **The Bad,** and The Ugly." [Malīs / Malus]

3. My team? I love the **Saints**! [Sanctōs / Sanctī]

4. I am short. I can't date a **tall woman.** [longa / longam]

5. **Handsome men** annoy me. [Pulcherī / Pulchrī]

6. **The Romans** are favored to win the race this year. [Romānī / Romānōs]

14-08 *Lectiō Prīma:* Comprehension.

Indicate whether each of the following statements from *Lectiō Prīma* is *Vērum* (true) or *Falsum* (false).

1. Astrologus mala Liciniae dixit.	V	F
2. Poētae Rōmānī multa dē Perseō in librīs narrant.	V	F
3. Perseus fīlia Iovis fuit.	V	F
4. Acrisius rex Argōrum fuit.	V	F
5. Iuppiter Perseum interficere cupit.	V	F
6. Danaē infantem in arcā inclūdit.	V	F
7. Infans in brācchiīs mātris territus est.	V	F
8. Danaē mare tranquillum facit.	V	F
9. Perseus et māter in marī quiescunt.	V	F
10. Quīdam Perseum et mātrem ad frātrem rēgis addūcunt.	V	F

14-09 I-Stem Rules.

Fill in the blanks with the correct words to make the rules complete and accurate. All rules refer to 3rd declension nouns only. Not every word from the *Thēsaurus Verbōrum* is used and none is used twice. Give the answers in the same order they appear in the chapter.

The parisyllabic rule: if the nominative ends in 1. _____ or 2. _____ and the genitive singular has the same number of 3. _____ as the 4. _____ case.

The double consonant rule: if the stem of the noun ends in two 5. _____.

The neuter rule: if the nominative ends in 6. _____, 7. _____, or 8. _____.

Thēsaurus Verbōrum

-al	consonants
-ar	letters
-e	nominative
-ēs	syllables
-is	vowels
-um	

14-10 Parisyllabic I-Stems.

Select all the parisyllabic i-stems from the list. You may want to review the rule before you begin. Not every word in the list is an i-stem.

_____ *aedēs, aedis* f. building, temple

_____ *animal, -ālis* n. animal

_____ *dens, dentis* m. tooth

_____ *exemplar, -āris* n. example

_____ *homō, hominis* m./f. person

_____ *hostis, hostis* m./f. enemy

_____ *ignis, ignis* m. fire

_____ *mare, maris* n. sea

_____ *mens, mentis* f. mind

_____ *mensis, mensis* f. month

_____ *mercātor, mercātōris* m. merchant

_____ *mons, montis* m. mountain

_____ *nōmen, nōminis* n. name

_____ *nox, noctis* f. night

_____ *opus, operis* n. work

_____ *pars, partis* f. part

_____ *rex, rēgis* m. king

_____ *soror, sorōris* f. sister

_____ *urbs, urbis* f. city

14-11 Double Consonant I-Stems. Select all the double consonant i-stems from the list. You may want to review the rule before you begin.

_____ *aedēs, aedis* f. building, temple

_____ *animal, -ālis* n. animal

_____ *dens, dentis* m. tooth

_____ *homō, hominis* m./f. person

_____ *exemplar, -āris* n. example

_____ *hostis, hostis* m./f. enemy

_____ *ignis, ignis* m. fire

_____ *mare, maris* n. sea

_____ *mens, mentis* f. mind

_____ *mensis, mensis* f. month

_____ *mercātor, mercātōris* m. merchant

_____ *mons, montis* m. mountain

_____ *nōmen, nōminis* n. name

_____ *nox, noctis* f. night

_____ *opus, operis* n. work

_____ *pars, partis* f. part

_____ *rex, rēgis* m. king

_____ *soror, sorōris* f. sister

_____ *urbs, urbis* f. city

14-12 Neuter I-Stems. Select all the neuter i-stems from the list. You may want to review the rule before you begin.

_____ *aedēs, aedis* f. building, temple

_____ *animal, -ālis* n. animal

_____ *dens, dentis* m. tooth

_____ *exemplar, -āris* n. example

_____ *homō, hominis* m./f. person

_____ *hostis, hostis* m./f. enemy

_____ *ignis, ignis* m. fire

_____ *mare, maris* n. sea

_____ *mens, mentis* f. mind

_____ *mensis, mensis* f. month

_____ *mercātor, mercātōris* m. merchant

_____ *mons, montis* m. mountain

_____ *nōmen, nōminis* n. name

_____ *nox, noctis* f. night

_____ *opus, operis* n. work

_____ *pars, partis* f. part

_____ *rex, rēgis* m. king

_____ *soror, sorōris* f. sister

_____ *urbs, urbis* f. city

14-13 I-Stems. Use the case ending of each 3rd declension noun to determine whether the word is an i-stem. Select *Sīc* (yes) or *Nōn* (no).

1. hostium
   Sīc   Nōn

2. ignium
   Sīc   Nōn

3. hominum
   Sīc   Nōn

4. nōmina
   Sīc   Nōn

5. maria
   Sīc   Nōn

6. noctium
   Sīc   Nōn

7. animālia
   Sīc   Nōn

8. fīnium
   Sīc   Nōn

9. rēgum
   Sīc   Nōn

10. frātrum
   Sīc   Nōn

14-14 *Lectiō Secunda: Quis est?* Use *Lectiō Secunda* to identify the person speaking in each sentence.

1. Iuppiter ad mē in nimbō aureō vēnit.
   a. Perseus   **b.** Acrisius   **c.** Danaē

2. Poētae multa dē mē in librīs narrant.
   a. Danaē   **b.** Perseus   **c.** Dictys

3. Frātrī rēgis meam fābulam dixī.
   a. Danaē   **b.** Perseus   **c.** Acrisius

4. Fīlia rēgis Acrisiī sum.
   a. Danaē   **b.** Perseus   **c.** Dictys

5. Frāter rēgis īnsulae Serīphī sum.
   a. Perseus   **b.** Acrisius   **c.** Dictys

6. Ūnā nocte in nimbō aureō vēnī.
   a. Iuppiter   **b.** Perseus   **c.** Acrisius

7. Infantem interficere voluī.
   a. Perseus   **b.** Acrisius   **c.** Dictys

8. Cupiō fīliō meō domum tūtam.
   a. Danaē   **b.** Perseus   **c.** Acrisius

14-15 *Verba Discenda.* Match the *Verbum Discendum* with its English meaning. Note that the Latin word is not always in the form you would find it in a dictionary.

1. *deum* ____
2. *infantis* ____
3. *fīnēs* ____
4. *noctibus* ____
5. *narrās* ____
6. *marium* ____
7. *tūtōrum* ____
8. *librīs* ____
9. *hostis* ____
10. *territa* ____
11. *interfēcit* ____
12. *agrō* ____
13. *rēgem* ____
14. *mensis* ____
15. *quiescere* ____

a. afraid
b. baby
c. book
d. end, territory
e. enemy
f. field
g. god
h. kill
i. king
j. month
k. night
l. rest
m. safe
n. sea
o. tell

14-16 How Closely Did You Read? Match the correct name or word to the description.

1. Perseus' father ____
2. He locked Perseus and his mother in a wooden chest ____
3. Perseus' mother ____
4. Protected Perseus and his mother on the island of Seriphos ____
5. An adjective used as a noun ____
6. A Greek pre-Socratic philosopher ____
7. A Roman feast celebrated in February ____
8. A Roman hill associated with the story of Romulus and Remus ____
9. The 3rd declension ending -ium is this kind of ending ____
10. The Roman historian who tells the story of Romulus, Remus and the she wolf. ____

a. Acrisius
b. Danae
c. Democritus
d. Dictys
e. Jupiter
f. Lupercalia
g. Palatinum
h. Livy
i. substantive
j. i-stem

14-17 Crossword Puzzle. Complete the puzzle with information from the chapter.

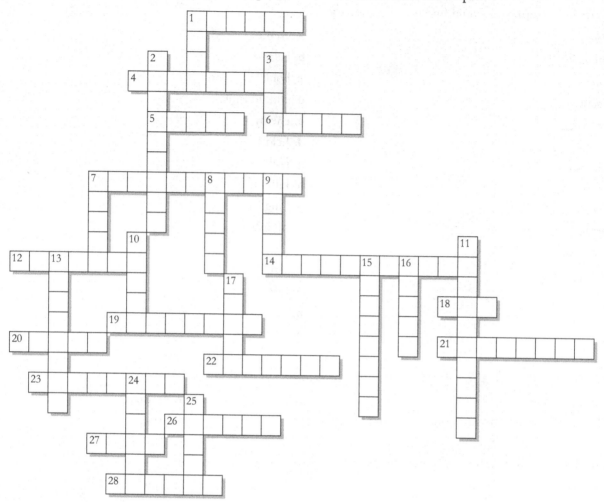

Across

1 – "Month"

4 – "To find"

5 – Romulus' twin

6 – "Seat, home"

7 – "To kill"

12 – "I rest."

14 – Adjective acting like a noun

18 – "Night"

19 – Hill in Rome with emperor's palaces

20 – "End"

21 – "Arm"

22 – He killed Medusa

23 – Cave of the wolf at Rome

26 – Rescued Perseus and Danae

27 – "Liber"

28 – "Enemy"

Down

1 – "Sea"

2 – Woman saved by Perseus

3 – "God"

7 – "Fire"

8 – 3rd declension noun whose genitive plural ends in *-ium*

9 – *Rex*, _____, m. king

10 – "Poet"

11 – Inventor of the term **atoms**

13 – 4th principal part of *inveniō*

15 – King of Argos, tried to kill Perseus

16 – "Safe"

17 – Perseus' mother

24 – Roman philosopher, orator, author, and politician

25 – "Books"

15 Frāter et Soror

15-01 Forming 3rd Declension Adjectives: 3 Terminations. Complete the chart by filling in the missing forms of *celer, celeris, celere*.

Case	Masculine	Feminine	Neuter
		Singular	
Nominative	celer	celeris	celere
Genitive	1. _____	2. _____	celeris
Dative	3. _____	4. _____	celerī
Accusative	5. _____	celerem	6. _____
Ablative	celerī	7. _____	8. _____
Vocative	9. _____	10. _____	11. _____
		Plural	
Nominative	celerēs	12. _____	13. _____
Genitive	14. _____	15. _____	celerium
Dative	16. _____	celeribus	17. _____
Accusative	18. _____	19. _____	celeria
Ablative	celeribus	20. _____	21. _____
Vocative	22. _____	23. _____	24. _____

15-02 Forming 3rd Declension Adjectives: 2 Terminations. Complete the chart by filling in the missing forms of *difficilis, difficile*.

Case	Masc./Fem.	Neuter
	Singular	
Nominative	difficilis	difficile
Genitive	1. _____	difficilis
Dative	2. _____	3. _____
Accusative	difficilem	4. _____
Ablative	difficilī	5. _____
Vocative	6. _____	difficile
	Plural	
Nominative	difficilēs	7. _____
Genitive	8. _____	difficilium
Dative	9. _____	10. _____
Accusative	11. _____	difficilia
Ablative	difficilibus	12. _____
Vocative	difficilēs	difficilia

15-03 Forming 3rd Declension Adjectives: 1 Termination.
Complete the chart by filling in the missing forms of *intellegens, intellegentis*.

Case	Masc./Fem.	Neuter
Singular		
Nominative	intellegens	intellegens
Genitive	1. _____	intellegentis
Dative	2. _____	intellegentī
Accusative	intelligentem	intellegens
Ablative	3. _____	4. _____
Vocative	5. _____	6. _____
Plural		
Nominative	7. _____	8. _____
Genitive	intellegentium	intellegentium
Dative	intellegentibus	intellegentibus
Accusative	9. _____	intellegentia
Ablative	intellegentibus	intellegentibus
Vocative	intellegentēs	10. _____

15-04 3rd Declension Adjectives: Endings.
Select the choice that correctly identifies the forms of *celer, celeris, celer*. Some forms can be more than one thing. You do not have to indicate gender.

1. *celeris*
 a. nom. sing. and nom. pl. **b.** nom. sing. and gen. sing. **c.** nom. sing. only

2. *celerī*
 a. gen. sing. and nom. pl. **b.** dat. sing. and nom. pl. **c.** dat. sing. and abl. sing.

3. *celere*
 a. abl. sing. only **b.** dat. sing. only **c.** nom. sing. and acc. sing.

4. *celerium*
 a. gen. pl. only **b.** acc. sing. only **c.** nom. sing. and acc. sing.

5. *celerēs*
 a. nom. pl. and acc. pl. **b.** dat. pl. and abl. pl. **c.** nom. pl. only

6. *celeria*
 a. abl. sing. only **b.** nom. pl. only **c.** nom. pl. and acc. pl.

7. *celeribus*
 a. dat. pl. only **b.** abl. pl. only **c.** dat. pl. and abl. pl.

8. *celer*
 a. nom. sing. only **b.** nom. sing. and acc. sing. **c.** nom. sing. and nom. pl.

15-05 GNC'ing! 3rd Declension Adjectives. Identify the GNC of each noun/adjective pair (use abbreviations). Each can be only one thing. Then translate the phrase into English. Follow the model.

	Gender	Number	Case	Translation
→ fēminae fortēs	*fem.*	*pl.*	*nom.*	*strong women*
1. fēminae fortis	_____	_____	_____	_____
2. fēminae fortī	_____	_____	_____	_____
3. puerōrum fortium	_____	_____	_____	_____
4. puerum fortem	_____	_____	_____	_____
5. puerī fortēs	_____	_____	_____	_____
6. puerōs fortes	_____	_____	_____	_____
7. puerī fortis	_____	_____	_____	_____

15-06 3rd Declension Adjectives: Manipulation. Change the number of the following noun/adjective pairs. If the phrase is singular, make it plural, and vice versa. Keep everything else the same. Follow the model.

→ puerōs fortēs   *puerum fortem*

1. puellae fortēs   _____
2. puellās fortēs   _____
3. filiam nōbilem   _____
4. vīna potentia   _____
5. hominem nōbilem   _____
6. hominī fortī   _____
7. homine fortī   _____
8. hominis celeris   _____

15-07 Find the Genitives. Select all the 3rd declension adjective genitive forms, singular and plural, from the list. Gender is **not** an issue in this exercise.

_____ forte   _____ fortia
_____ fortem   _____ fortibus
_____ fortēs   _____ fortis
_____ fortī   _____ fortium

15-08 Find the Datives. Select all the 3rd declension adjective dative forms, singular and plural, from the list. Gender is **not** an issue in this exercise.

_____ forte   _____ fortia
_____ fortem   _____ fortibus
_____ fortēs   _____ fortis
_____ fortī   _____ fortium

15-09 Find the Accusatives. Select all the 3rd declension adjective accusative forms, singular and plural, from the list. Gender **is** an issue in this exercise.

_____ forte		_____ fortia	
_____ fortem		_____ fortibus	
_____ fortēs		_____ fortis	
_____ fortī		_____ fortium	

15-10 GNC'ing with 3rd Declension Adjectives. The following passage has English words numbered and marked in **bold**. Each one represents a 3rd declension adjective. Select the choice that best represents what the word would be in Latin. For gender, use English conventions—masculine and feminine for living creatures; neuter for things.

I like to read everything, but fairy tales tend to be the same. In **every** (1) _____ (omnia – omnibus – omnī) kingdom there lives a **powerful** (2) _____ (potens – potentis – potentem) king. We are told the name of his **sad** (3) _____ (tristis – tristī – tristem) daughter whom **all** (4) _____ (omnis – omnem – omnēs) the young men want to marry. But the king won't give her just **to a noble** (5) _____ (nōbilī – nōbilem – nōbile) youth. First we see a **brave** (6) _____ (fortis – forte – fortem) young man who fails and is killed by the breath of **powerful** (7) _____ (potentis – potentibus – potentium) dragons. Another **noble** (8) _____ (nōbile – nōbilis – nōbilem) youth appears and undertakes the **serious** (9) _____ (gravem – grave – gravis) task set for him, but he too dies. Finally, we are told about (_dē_) an **intelligent** (10) _____ (intellegens – intellegentem – intellegentī) young lad who wins the day as well as the **noble** (11) _____ (nōbilem – nōbilī – nōbilis) princess. They live happily ever after, of course, but the dragons are pretty **sad** (12) _____ (tristis – tristibus – tristēs).

15-11 3rd Declension Substantives. Match each English sentence with the Latin sentence that best translates it. Pay particular attention to the substantives (in **bold**). Unusual vocabulary can be figured out from context.

1. **Fortēs** fortūna adiuvat. _____
2. **Intellegens** semper laetus est. _____
3. **Omnī** suum. _____
4. **Difficilia** semper nōbīs erunt. _____
5. **Potentēs** nihil timent. _____
6. **Omnēs** nōn **omnia** facere possunt. _____

    a. A smart man is a happy man.
    b. Everyone can't do everything.
    c. Fortune favors the brave.
    d. The mighty have no fears.
    e. To each his own.
    f. We'll always have problems.

15-12 GNC'ing! 3rd Declension Adjectives with 3rd Declension Nouns. Supply the correct form of the adjective in parentheses to modify each 3rd declension noun. Follow the model.

→ rēgum (fortis)   *fortium*

1. sorōrem (tristis)   _____
2. ōrātiōnēs (gravis)   _____
3. amōre (dulcis)   _____
4. hostium (crūdēlis)   _____
5. hominibus (potens)   _____
6. nōmina (nōbilis)   _____
7. mātrum (intellegens)   _____
8. mare (potens)   _____
9. animālia (fortis)   _____
10. iuvene (celer)   _____

15-13 GNC'ing! 3rd Declension Adjectives with 1st/2nd Declension Nouns. Supply the correct form of the adjective in parentheses to modify each 1st or 2nd declension noun. Some questions have two possible answers. When listing multiple answers, list them in the order they would appear in a chart. A genitive singular answer will come before a nnomiinative plural answer. Follow the model.

→ virī (fortis)   *fortis* (gen. sing.) or *fortēs* (nom. pl.)

1. vīna (dulcis)   _____
2. puellā (nōbilis)   _____
3. puerī (tristis)   _____ or _____
4. viam (facilis)   _____
5. fēminīs (intellegens) _____
6. amīcōrum (crūdēlis) _____
7. virōs (potens)   _____
8. discipulō (fortis)   _____
9. verba (fortis)   _____
10. vītae (difficilis) _____ or _____ or _____

15-14 GNC'ing! 3rd Declension Adjectives with Mixed Declension Nouns. Choose the correct form of the adjective to GNC with each noun.

1. ōrātiōnēs
   a. intellegens   **b.** intellegentem   **c.** intellegentēs

2. soror
   a. fēlix   **b.** fēlīcis   **c.** fēlīcem

3. familia
   a. omnis   **b.** omnia   **c.** omne

4. virōs
   a. tristis   **b.** tristibus   **c.** tristēs

5. sorōre
   a. dulcis   **b.** dulcī   **c.** dulce

6. hostium

    a. crūdēlis   **b.** crūdēlium   **c.** crūdēlēs

7. familiārum

    a. omnis   **b.** omnium   **c.** omne

8. poētās

    a. nōbilis   **b.** nōbilem   **c.** nōbilēs

9. Rōmānō

    a. nōbilī   **b.** nōbile   **c.** nōbilium

10. ancillae

    a. dulcī   **b.** dulce   **c.** dulcibus

15-15 Which Form? Mixed Declensions. Select the form of the adjective that properly GNC's with the noun. Only one choice is the same GNC as the noun.

1. magistrī   [fortis / forte]

2. ancillae   [crūdēlēs / crudēle]

3. rēgum   [intellegentium / intellegentem]

4. sorōre   [pulchrae / pulchrā]

5. adulescentī   [laetō / laetī]

6. animal   [fēlix / fēlīce]

7. puerī   [celerī / celeris]

8. fīlia   [omnī / omnis]

9. parentum   [bonum / bonōrum]

10. sīmiās   [laetae / laetōs]

15-16 From Adverbs to Adjectives. Based on the meaning of the Latin adjectives you know, select the best description for the adverbs given.

1. intellegenter _____   **a.** the way someone ran

2. difficiliter _____   **b.** how he did something hard

3. fortiter _____   **c.** how she treated the trial

4. graviter _____   **d.** the way Superman does anything

5. potenter _____   **e.** the way Einstein thought

6. celeriter _____   **f.** the way he fought in battle

15-17 How Closely Did You Read? Match the phrase or statement with the word that it describes.

1. The unwritten code of behavior by which Romans were taught to live _____   **a.** Arpinum

2. The Latin word for "an ordered life" _____   **b.** Catiline

3. The Latin word for "diligence" _____   **c.** *disciplīna*

4. The Latin word for "economy" _____   **d.** *frūgālitās*

5. The Latin word for "seriousness" _____   **e.** *gravitās*

6. The Latin term for "a sense of obligation" _____   **f.** *industria*

7. The Latin term for "manliness, excellence" _____   **g.** *mōs maiōrum*

8. Cicero's birthplace _____   **h.** *officium*

9. Cicero owned a favorite villa here _____   **i.** Tusculum

10. As consul, Cicero accused him of treason _____   **j.** *virtūs*

15-18 *Verba Discenda:* **Missing Parts.** Write in the missing information from the dictionary entry of these *verba discenda.*

1. *legō, legere,* _____, *lectum* gather, choose; read
2. *amor,* _____ m. love
3. *corpus, corporis* _____ body
4. *iuvenis,* _____ m./f. youth
5. *vox, vōcis* _____ voice
6. *vērē* _____
7. _____ when
8. *fortis,* _____ strong, brave
9. *tristis, triste* _____
10. *omnis, omne* _____ (pl.) all

15-19 *Verba Discenda:* **Meanings.** Match the English translation to the Latin word. Synonyms may be used for the definition given in the *Verba Discenda* to encourage you to learn the word more thoroughly.

1. *amor* _____
2. *celer* _____
3. *corpus* _____
4. *cum* _____
5. *difficilis* _____
6. *fortis* _____
7. *gravis* _____
8. *intellegens* _____
9. *iuvenis* _____
10. *legō* _____
11. *māior* _____
12. *mōs* _____
13. *nec* _____
14. *nōbilis* _____
15. *omnis* _____
16. *potens* _____
17. *tristis* _____
18. *vērē* _____
19. *vērus* _____
20. *vox* _____

a. and not
b. body
c. choose
d. custom
e. every
f. fast
g. greater
h. hard
i. heavy
j. love
k. noble
l. powerful
m. sad
n. smart
o. strong
p. true
q. truly
r. voice
s. when
t. youth

15-20 Crossword Puzzle. Complete the puzzle with information from the chapter.

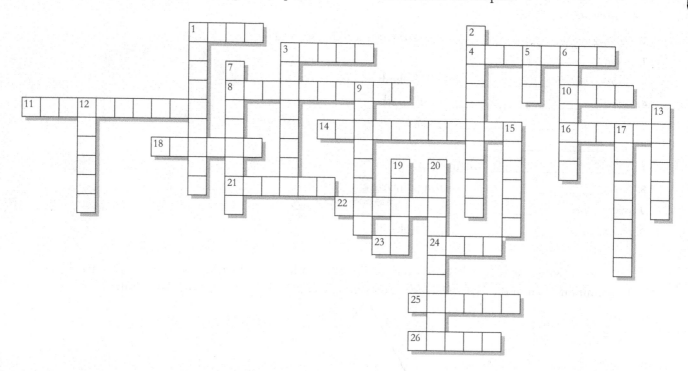

Across

1 – Adverbs based on 3ʳᵈ declension adjectives end in ____

3 – "Swift"

4 – "Sense of obligation, duty"

8 – Question asked more for effect than to learn something

10 – "Truly"

11 – "Young man"

14 – *Potens, -entis* is a 1 ____ adjective

16 – "Our"

18 – "Strong"

21 -- Carried his father from burning Troy

22 – "Manliness, excellence"

23 – 3ʳᵈ declension adjective m./f., accusative singular ending

24 – 3ʳᵈ declension dative plural ending

25 – Consul in 63 B.C.

26 – Latin word "majority" is derived from this word

Down

1 – "____ence"

2 – "R____ code of conduct"

3 – His p____ as foiled by Cicero

5 – 3ʳᵈ decl____n adjectives, genitive plural end____

6 – Latin word "juvenile" is derived from this word

7 – "Seriousness"

9 – "*Corpus,* ____ n. body"

12 – "To read"

13 – "Heavy"

15 – "Neither … nor"

17 – Cicero wrote his *Disputations* here

19 – 3ʳᵈ declension adjectives use these endings

20 – "An ordered life"

In Cēnā

16-01 Formulas for Forming the Future Tense. Fill in the blanks with the word from the *Thēsaurus Verbōrum* that makes the statement true. All words are used, but none is used twice.

Thēsaurus Verbōrum

1st

2nd

-am, -ēs, -et, -ēmus, -ētis, -ent

-bō, -bis, -bit, -bimus, -bitis, -bunt

-ō

present

-re

short present

A. To form the future tense of 1st and 2nd conjugation verbs:

Take the (1)_____ stem, which is formed by dropping the
(2)_____ of the (3)_____ principal part. To this stem you
add the endings (4)_____

B. To form the future tense of 3rd and 4th conjugation verbs:

Take the (5)_____ stem, which is formed by dropping the
(6)_____ of the (7)_____ principal part. To this stem
you add the endings (8)_____

16-02 Forming the Future Tense. Complete the chart with the missing future tense forms of *vocō, scrībō,* and *dormiō*.

1st Declension	3rd Declension	4th Declension
	Singular	
vocābō	4. _____	7. _____
vocābis	scrībēs	8. _____
1. _____	scrībet	dormiet
	Plural	
2. _____	5. _____	dormiēmus
3. _____	scrībētis	9. _____
vocābunt	6. _____	10. _____

16-03 Identifying Tenses. Select the correct tense of the given Latin verb. Is it present or future?

1. *capiet*	present	future	
2. *cupiunt*	present	future	
3. *dormiēmus*	present	future	
4. *audit*	present	future	
5. *videt*	present	future	
6. *dīcet*	present	future	
7. *habēs*	present	future	
8. *audiēs*	present	future	
9. *dormiētis*	present	future	
10. *habent*	present	future	

16-04 Identifying Future Tense Verbs. Select all the future tense verbs in this list. The list contains present, ıre, and perfect tense verbs.

_____ agam

_____ agētis

_____ dīcēs

_____ dīcimus

_____ didicērunt

_____ discent

_____ discis

_____ ēgimus

_____ faciēmus

_____ facit

_____ fēcit

_____ pōnēmus

_____ portābimus

_____ portant

_____ portāvērunt

_____ posuit

_____ vidēbitis

_____ vidēs

_____ vīdistis

16-05 Identifying Perfect Tense Verbs: Review. Select all the perfect tense verbs in this list. The list contains present, future, and perfect tense verbs.

_____ agam

_____ agētis

_____ dīcēs

_____ dīcimus

_____ didicērunt

_____ discent

_____ discis

_____ dixit

_____ ēgimus

_____ faciēmus

_____ facit

_____ fēcit

_____ pōnēmus

_____ portābimus

_____ portant

_____ portāvērunt

_____ posuit

_____ vidēbitis

_____ vidēs

_____ vīdistis

16-06 Identifying Present Tense Verbs: Review.

Select all the present tense verbs in this list. The list contains present, future, and perfect tense verbs.

_____ agam   _____ facit
_____ agētis   _____ fēcit
_____ dīcēs   _____ ponēmus
_____ dīcimus   _____ portābimus
_____ didicērunt   _____ portant
_____ discent   _____ portāvērunt
_____ discis   _____ posuit
_____ dixit   _____ vidēbitis
_____ ēgimus   _____ vidēs
_____ faciēmus   _____ vīdistis

16-07 Distinguishing Three Tenses: Latin to English.

You now know three tenses, and it is important to be able to distinguish between them. Select the correct translation for the given verb.

1. *capis* _____   a. you saw
2. *capiēs* _____   b. you are sleeping
3. *cēpistī* _____   c. you have
4. *dūcēs* _____   d. you have led
5. *duxistī* _____   e. you lead
6. *dūcis* _____   f. you seize
7. *vidēbitis* _____   g. you seized
8. *habēs* _____   h. you will have
9. *dormiēs* _____   i. you will lead
10. *dormīs* _____   j. you will see
11. *habēbitis* _____   k. you will seize
12. *vīdistī* _____   l. you will sleep

16-08 Distinguishing Three Tenses: English to Latin.

You now know three tenses, and it is important to be able to distinguish between them. Select the correct translation for the given verb.

1. you related _____   a. *capiēs*
2. you run _____   b. *capis*
3. you seize _____   c. *cucurristī*
4. you ran _____   d. *currēs*
5. you will seize _____   e. *curris*
6. you will run _____   f. *legēs*
7. you relate _____   g. *legis*
8. you will relate _____   h. *lēgistī*
9. you will read _____   i. *narrābitis*
10. you are reading _____ j. *narrātis*
11. you have read _____   k. *narrāvistī*

16-09 Translating Present and Future Tenses: Regular and Irregular Verbs. Choose the correct translation for each of the following verbs. Pay careful attention to tense.

1. *ībunt*
   a. they go
   b. he will go
   c. they will go
   d. they go

2. *eris*
   a. he will be
   b. you are
   c. you will be
   d. you all will be

3. *circumambulābitis*
   a. you walk around
   b. you all walk around
   c. you all will walk around
   d. they will walk around

4. *dīcent*
   a. they say
   b. he says
   c. he will say
   d. they will say

5. *portābimus*
   a. we will carry
   b. we are carrying
   c. we carry
   d. we do carry

6. *adiuvat*
   a. he helps
   b. she will help
   c. they will help
   d. they help

7. *dormiēmus*
   a. we sleep
   b. we are sleeping
   c. we will sleep
   d. we do sleep

8. *audiētis*
   a. you hear
   b. you all are hearing
   c. you are hearing
   d. you all will hear

9. *dēbēmus*
   a. we ought
   b. we will have to
   c. we will owe
   d. they must

10. *scrībit*
    a. he will write
    b. she writes
    c. she will be writing
    d. they write

16-10 Comprehension: *Lectiō Prīma*. The following questions are based on *Lectiō Prīma*. Answer them with short Latin sentences.

→ Quid familia exspectat in trīclīniō?
   Familia cēnam exspectat.

1. Ubi Servīlius et Marcus et Lūcius sunt? _____

2. Ubi Caecilia et Servīlia sedent? _____

3. Ubi servī stant? _____

4. Quis fābulās bene scrībit? _____

5. Quis fortasse fābulās bene narrābit? _____

6. Cūr mox familia cibum nōn habēbit? _____

7. Quis est Valgius Rūfus? _____

8. Ubi Marcus mox ōrātiōnēs habēbit? _____

16-11 Irregular Verb Review: All Tenses. Translate the following forms of *sum, eō, volō, nōlō,* and *mālō*. Be careful! We have mixed the tenses.

1. *eris*

   a. you are   **b.** you were   **c.** you will be

2. *poterō*

   a. I am able   **b.** I was able   **c.** I will be able

3. *ībunt*

   a. they are going   **b.** they went   **c.** they will go

4. *potuimus*

   a. we are able   **b.** we have been able   **c.** we will be able

5. *volētis*

   a. you want   **b.** you wanted   **c.** you will want

6. *nōlunt*

   a. they don't want   **b.** they didn't want   **c.** they will not want

7. *fuistis*

   a. you are   **b.** you have been   **c.** you will be

8. *mālent*

   a. they prefer   **b.** they preferred   **c.** they will prefer

16-12 Irregular Futures: Change the Number. Change the number of the following irregular futures, from singular to plural or vice versa. Follow the model.

    → erimus   *erō*

1. ībit _____

2. eritis _____

3. volam _____

4. aderimus _____

5. mālent _____

6. volēs _____

7. poterit _____

8. nōlet _____

16-13 *Iullus Antonius et al.* Select the correct information concerning the life of Iullus Antonius and other historical events and figures. All dates are B.C.

1. He was Iullus' father.

   a. Julius Caesar   **b.** Pompey   **c.** Marc Antony

2. It was the year Iullus was born.

   a. 45   **b.** 31   **c.** 2

3. She was Iullus' mother.

   a. Fulvia   **b.** Octavia   **c.** Julia

4. She was Iullus' stepmother.

   a. Fulvia   **b.** Octavia   **c.** Julia

5. Octavia's relationship to Augustus.

   a. sister   **b.** mother   **c.** mistress

6. Iullus' affair with her caused him to fall out of favor with Augustus.

   a. Fulvia   **b.** Julia   **c.** Octavia

16-14 Comprehension: *Lectiō Secunda*. Select the speaker of each of the following quotations derived from *Lectiō Secunda*. Consider what is being said, and you will easily know the speaker.

1. *"Crās, cum Marcō, rursus ad Cordum ībō!"*
Servilius   Servilia

2. *"Ēheu! Quid dīcis? Sed quis marītus meus erit?"*
Servilius   Servilia

3. *"Hodiē marītum tibi lēgī."*
Servilius   Servilia

4. *"Cum Cordō in hortōs Maecēnātis nōn ībis. Rē vērā, cum Cordō numquam eris."*
Servilius   Servilia

5. *"Mox eris mātrōna!"*
Servilius   Servilia

6. *"Nōlīte anxiī esse, mī pārentēs, ancillae meae aderunt et nōbīscum ambulābunt!"*
Servilius   Servilia

7. *"Egō et Iullus Antonius multa prō rēpublicā efficere poterimus!"*
Servilius   Servilia

8. *"Nōn Iullī sed Cordī uxor erō!"*
Servilius   Servilia

16-15 *Verba Discenda*. Match the Latin word with the best English translation.

1. *adiuvō* ____		**a.** a lot, much
2. *apud* ____		**b.** again
3. *ars* ____		**c.** alas! oh no!
4. *diū* ____		**d.** art, skill
5. *ēheu* ____		**e.** at the house of
6. *exspectō* ____		**f.** await, wait for
7. *haud* ____		**g.** by no means
8. *labor* ____		**h.** famous
9. *magis* ____		**i.** for a long time
10. *marītus* ____		**j.** help
11. *mensa* ____		**k.** husband
12. *multum* ____		**l.** more, rather
13. *nimium* ____		**m.** parent
14. *ōrātiō* ____		**n.** rhetorical
15. *parens* ____		**o.** speech
16. *praeclārus* ____		**p.** table
17. *rhētor* ____		**q.** teacher of rhetoric
18. *rhētoricus* ____		**r.** too much
19. *rursus* ____		**s.** work, labor

16-16 *Verba Discenda*: **Derivatives.** Use your knowldege of the *Verba Discenda* for this chapter to figure out the meanings of these English words.

1. commensal _____
2. peroration _____
3. mesa _____
4. premarital _____
5. elaborate _____
6. laborious _____
7. parentage _____
8. multiparous _____
9. nimiety _____
10. collaboration _____

a. eating at the same table
b. having borne many children
c. high, flat, table-like land
d. one's descent from ancestors
e. preceding marriage
f. requiring a great deal of work
g. surfeit, overabundance
h. the concluding part of a speech
i. worked out with great care
j. working together

16-17 **Pesky Little Words.** What would the Latin be for the word or phrase in **bold**? Fill in the blank with the letter of the appropriate word.

a. apud (+ acc.)
b. diū
c. ēheu
d. haud
e. magis
f. multum
g. nimium
h. rursus

The other day Caecilia was **at** (1)_____ her friend's house and they talked for a **long time** (2)_____.

"Did you hear?" the friend said. "Claudius Bibulus has **greatly** (3)_____ angered the emperor **again** (4)_____

"**By no means** (5)_____ did I hear," said Caecila. "What did he do?"

"Well," the friend continued, "as usual, he was drinking, but this time he drank **too much** (6)_____ and was **more** (7)_____ reckless than usual. He decided to visit Octavia, Augustus' sister and fell into her impluvium."

"**Oh no!** (8)_____!" Caecilia exclaimed. "That just might be the end of him!"

16-18 **How Closely Did You Read?** Match the term with its identification.

1. Seneca the Elder _____
2. Latium _____
3. Iullus Antonius _____
4. Valgius Rufus _____
5. Marc Antony's famous lover _____
6. *suāsōriae* _____
7. *contrōversiae* _____
8. Augustus' sister, married Marc Antony _____

a. Author of speeches and legal arguments
b. Servilius engages his daughter to him
c. Cleopatra
d. Fictional law cases and legal arguments
e. Marcus' rhetoric teacher
f. Persuasive speeches
g. Octavia
h. The region around Rome

16-19 Crossword Puzzle. Complete the puzzle with information from the chapter.

Across

2 – "By no means"

3 – "Husband"

4 – "A lot"

7 – Latin town known today as Palestrina

12 – Fictional law cases assigned to rhetoric students

13 – Octavian's scandalous daughter

15 – "Oh no!"

16 – "Exspectō"

18 – "Again"

19 – "For a long time"

21 – Persuasive speeches assigned to rhetoric students

24 – The stem for the future forms of *sum*

Down

1 – Stem for the future of 3rd and 4th conjugation verbs

5 – The region around Rome

6 – Stem for the future of 1st and 2nd conjugation verbs

8 – "At the house of"

9 – Iullus Antonius' stepmother

10 – "Famous"

11 – "Too much"

14 – Case used with *apud*

17 – 3rd principal part of *adiuvō*

20 – "More, rather"

22 – "Skill, art"

23 – Marcus' rhetoric teacher

17   Dē Amōre et Lūdīs

17-01 All About Participles. Select the answer that best completes the statement concerning present active participles.

1. The present active participle is translated into English using _____.
   a. "to"   **b.** "having been"   **c.** "-ing"

2. All participles are verbal _____.
   a. nouns   **b.** adjectives   **c.** adverbs

3. All infinitives are verbal _____.
   a. nouns   **b.** adjectives   **c.** adverbs

4. Present active participles are declined like what?
   a. 2-1-2 adjectives   **b.** 3rd declension adjectives   **c.** neither a nor b

5. Present active participles can be viewed as _____.
   a. 1-termination adjectives   **b.** 2-termination adjectives   **c.** 3-termination adjectives

6. The only present active participles that do not end in *-ēns* are from what conjugation?_____
   a. 1st **b.** 2nd **c.** 3rd **d.** 4th

17-02 Participles and Their Verbs. Indicate the verb from which each of the listed participles must derive. This exercise is designed to help you work with participles when you see them in a passage. NOTE: Some of the choices are not real verbs. Only one choice is possible for each participle.

1. habitāns:
   a. habitō, -āre   **b.** habiteō, -ēre   **c.** habitō, -ere

2. habentēs:
   a. habō, -āre   **b.** habeō, -ēre   **c.** habiō, -īre

3. interficiēns:
   a. interficō, -āre   **b.** interficeō, -ēre   **c.** interficiō, -ere

4. manentibus:
   a. manō, -āre   **b.** maneō, -ēre   **c.** maniō, -īre

5. iacientēs:
   a. iacō, -āre   **b.** iaceō, -ēre   **c.** iaciō, -ere

6. cadentis:
   a. cadō, -āre   **b.** cadō, -ere   **c.** cadiō, cadīre

17-03 Participles. For each participle ending given, select the conjugations from which it can come. If there is more than one possible answer, select them all. Follow the model.

→ -iēns
  a. 1st   **b.** 2nd   **c.** 3rd regular   **d.** *3rd -iō*   **e.** *4th*

(the *-i* in the participle's ending rules out the 2nd and 3rd regular conjugations)

1. -ēns
  a. 1st   **b.** 2nd   **c.** 3rd regular   **d.** 3rd *-iō*   **e.** 4th

2. -entēs
  a. 1st   **b.** 2nd   **c.** 3rd regular   **d.** 3rd *-iō*   **e.** 4th

3. -āns
  a. 1st   **b.** 2nd   **c.** 3rd regular   **d.** 3rd *-iō*   **e.** 4th

4. -ientis
  a. 1st   **b.** 2nd   **c.** 3rd regular   **d.** 3rd *-iō*   **e.** 4th

5. -antem
  a. 1st   **b.** 2nd   **c.** 3rd regular   **d.** 3rd *-iō*   **e.** 4th

6. -entibus
  a. 1st   **b.** 2nd   **c.** 3rd regular   **d.** 3rd *-iō*   **e.** 4th

17-04 Participles: Case and Number Possibilities. Fill in the blank with the appropriate case and number of each participle, using the abbreviations provided. List all possibilities. In one case you are given the gender. Follow the model.

Abbreviations

nom.   sing.
gen.   pl.
dat.
acc.
abl.

→ habentibus   *dat. pl., abl. pl.*

1. habentem _____

2. habēns n. _____

3. habentium _____

4. habentī _____

5. habentia _____

6. habentis _____

7. habentēs _____

8. habentibus _____

17-05 Participles: Case and Number, English. What would the case of the participle in **bold** be if the sentence were in Latin? Fill in the blank with the appropriate case and number, using the abbreviations provided.

Abbreviations

nom.   sing.
gen.   pl.
dat.
acc.
abl.

Walking (1)_____ in the park, George saw the monkey **swinging** (2)_____ through the trees. But the monkey did not know the name of the man **walking** (3)_____ in the park. Still, he saw the man **walking** (4)_____ and wanted to meet him. So the monkey, **swinging** (5)_____ through the trees, came close and gave a banana to the **smiling** (6)_____ man, and the two became fast friends. Now, almost any day, you can see the monkey and the man **walking** (7)_____ in the park, although sometimes they both travel faster, **swinging** (8)_____ through the trees.

17-06 Participle Agreement: English. As verbal adjectives, participles modify nouns. Determine first what noun the participle (in **bold**) is modifying. Then select the case and number the participle has to be in. Follow the model.

→ Give the butter to the cook **making** the cake.
nominative / genitive / *dative* / accusative / ablative
singular / plural
(**cook** is an indirect object and is singular; therefore you select "dative" and "singular.")

1. The flag, **flying** in the breeze, was visible for miles.
nominative / genitive / dative / accusative / ablative
singular / plural

2. The policeman caught the **speeding** driver.
nominative / genitive / dative / accusative / ablative
singular / plural

3. Do you know the name of that one **dancing** over there?
nominative / genitive / dative / accusative / ablative
singular / plural

4. The voices of the **singing** children were sweet.
nominative / genitive / dative / accusative / ablative
singular / plural

5. I gave water to all 526 people **running** in the marathon.
nominative / genitive / dative / accusative / ablative
singular / plural

6. Never stop to chat with **raving** maniacs.
nominative / genitive / dative / accusative / ablative
singular / plural

17-07 Participles: Case and Number, Latin. Select the correct Latin participle that substitutes for the word or phrase in **bold**. All are forms of the verb *intrō, -āre*. Notice as you go the different ways you can translate a present participle.

1. The people saw Augustus **entering** the Forum.
   a. intrāns   b. intrantis   c. intrantī   d. intrantem

2. Licinia, who loved Augustus, gave a gift to him **as he entered** the Forum.
   a. intrāns   b. intrantis   c. intrantī   d. intrantem

3. She wanted to hear the words of Augustus **as he entered** the Forum.
   a. intrāns   b. intrantis   c. intrantī   d. intrantem

4. **Entering** the Forum, Augustus attracted quite a crowd.
   a. intrāns   b. intrantis   c. intrantī   d. intrantem

5. A huge crowd walked with Augustus **as he entered** the Forum.
   a. intrāns   b. intrantis   c. intrantī   d. intrantem

6. **Entering** the Forum, Lucius and Marcus caught sight of Augustus.
   a. intrāns   b. intrantēs   c. intrantium   d. intrantem

7. Augustus did not notice Lucius and Marcus **entering** the Forum.
   a. intrāns   b. intrantēs   c. intrantium   d. intrantibus

8. Augustus did not hear the greetings of Lucius and Marcus **as they entered** the Forum.
   a. intrāns   b. intrantēs   c. intrantium   d. intrantibus

9. But the guard did speak harshly to Lucius and Marcus **while they entered** the Forum.
   a. intrāns   b. intrantēs   c. intrantium   d. intrantibus

10. Horatia walked with Lucius and Marcus **as they entered** the Forum.
   a. intrāns   b. intrantēs   c. intrantium   d. intrantibus

17-08 GNC'ing! Participles in Latin. Fill in the proper form of the participle in each sentence (based on *Lectiō Prīma*). Be sure to GNC with the word in **bold**! Follow the model.

→ Post cēnam **Servīlia** in cubiculō sōla _____*lacrimāns*_____ sedet. (lacrimō)

1. **Servīlia** sōlāciolum suī dolōris _____ rīdet. (petō)

2. Servīlia **passerem** _____ in gremiō tenet. (sedeō)

3. **Iullum** in viā _____ numquam vīdī! (ambulō)

4. Numquam vōcem **Iullī** _____ audīvī. (dīcō)

5. Passer nihil **puellae** _____ dīcit. (lacrimō)

6. Servīlia rīdet per **lacrimās** _____. (cadō)

17-09 GNC'ing! Participial Substantives. The words marked in **bold** are participles acting as substantives. Choose the correct translation for each participle. Pay attention to number and gender, often shown by an adjective.

1. **Labōrāns** in culīnā fessus est.
   a. the men working
   b. the man working
   c. the woman working
   d. the women working

2. **Labōrāns** in culīnā fessa est.
   a. the men working
   b. the man working
   c. the woman working
   d. the women working

3. **Labōrantēs** in culīnā fessī sunt.
   a. the men working
   b. the man working
   c. the woman working
   d. the women working

4. **Labōrantēs** in culīnā fessae sunt.
   a. the men working
   b. the man working
   c. the woman working
   d. the women working

5. **Ambulantēs** in culīnam īrātae sunt.
   a. the men walking
   b. the man walking
   c. the woman walking
   d. the women walking

6. **Ambulāns** in viā īrāta est.
   a. the men walking
   b. the man walking
   c. the woman walking
   d. the women walking

7. **Ambulantēs** ad Forum fessī sunt.
   a. the men walking
   b. the man walking
   c. the woman walking
   d. the women walking

8. **Ambulāns** in viā īrātus est.
   a. the men walking
   b. the man walking
   c. the woman walking
   d. the women walking

17-10 Translating Participial Substantives. Select the correct translation for each sentence.

1. Passer nihil **lacrimantī** dīcit.
   a. Crying, she says nothing to the sparrow.
   b. The sparrow says nothing to her as she cries.

2. **Ambulantem** in viā numquam vīdī!
   a. I never saw him walking in the road.
   b. Walking in the road, I never saw him.

3. Sōlāciolum suī dolōris **petēns** rīdet.
   a. She laughs, seeking solace for her sorrow.
   b. Laughing, she seeks solace for her sorrow.

4. Sōlāciolum **lacrimantī** fēmina dedit.
   a. The woman, crying, gave her solace.
   b. The woman gave solace to the one crying.

5. Vōcem **lacrimantis** omnēs audīvērunt.
   a. Crying, everybody heard the voice.
   b. Everybody heard the voice of her as she cried.

6. Numquam **lacrimāns** Cordum in viā vīdī.
   a. I never saw Cordus crying in the road.
   b. Crying, I never saw Cordus in the road.

17-11 *"Quis Est?" Lectiō Prīma:* **Comprehension.** Identify in Latin the person or thing described in each sentence based on *Lectiō Prīma*. Use the *Thēsaurus Nōminum*. Be careful, because the order of the questions does not follow the sequence of events in the narrative. Follow the model.

Thēsaurus Nōminum

Catullus
Cordus
Iullus
Passer
Servīlia

→ Quis carmen fāmōsum dē morte Lesbiae passeris scrīpsit? *Catullus*

1. Quis circumsiliēns et pīpiāns nihil puellae lacrimantī dīcit? _____

2. Quis cor suum Cordō adulescentī iam dedit? _____

3. Quis cor suum virō senī numquam dabit? _____

4. Quis cūrās tristēs puellae levat? _____

5. Quis dē Lesbiā multa carmina amātōria scripsit? _____

6. Quis est sōlāciolum Servīliae dolōris? _____

7. Quis in domō istīus senis numquam habitābit? _____

8. Quis in Servīliae gremiō sedet? _____

9. Quis Lesbiam amāvit? _____

10. Quis passerī prīmum digitum dat? _____

11. Quis plūs quam trīgintā quinque annōs habet? _____

12. Quis post cēnam in cubiculō lacrimāns sedet? _____

17-12 **UNUS NAUTA Words: Forms.** Select the possible case and number combinations for each word. Do not forget to consider gender as you decide. If more than one answer is possible, select them all. Follow the model.

→ utrō **a.** dat. sing. **b.** *abl. sing.*

1. ullī
  a. nom. pl.   **b.** dat. sing.   **c.** gen. sing.

2. ullīus
  a. dat. sing.   **b.** gen. sing.   **c.** dat. pl.

3. neutra
  a. nom. sing.   **b.** nom. pl.   **c.** abl. sing.

4. ūnum
  a. nom. sing.   **b.** acc. sing.   **c.** gen. pl.

5. alia
  a. nom. sing.   **b.** dat. sing.   **c.** nom. pl.

6. utrae
  a. nom. pl.   **b.** gen. sing.   **c.** dat. sing.

17-13 UNUS NAUTA Words. Match the phrases containing UNUS NAUTA words to their translations.

1. sōla familia _____
2. illa ipsa familia _____
3. illa familia _____
4. illīus familiae _____
5. nūllī aliī familiae _____
6. neutrī familiae _____
7. nūllam familiam _____
8. familia ipsa _____
9. familiae sōlīus _____
10. ūnī familiae _____

a. the family itself
b. of the family alone
c. of that family
d. that very family
e. that family
f. to neither family
g. no family
h. to one family
i. the only family
j. to no other family

17-14 *Lectiō Secunda*: Comprehension. Use both *lectiōnēs* to answer the following questions in Latin. Base your answers on the story (not on the Catullus' poems), and answer in complete Latin sentences. Follow the model.

Thēsaurus Verbōrum

quis? (singular)	who?
quī? (plural)	who?
quid?	what?
qualia?	what kind of?

→ Quis sōlāciolum suī dolōris petēns rīdet?
Servīlia, sōlāciolum petēns, rīdet.

1. Quis magna mūnera in amphitheātrō dabit? _____
2. Quid Marcus et Lūcius in amphitheātrō vidēbunt? _____
3. Qualia animālia in mūneribus erunt? _____
4. Quī cum animālibus exōticīs pugnābunt? _____
5. Quid hominēs advenientēs māne ad amphitheātrum habēbunt? _____
6. Quis negōtium multum sed parvum ōtium habet? _____

17-15 How Closely Did You Read? Select the term that is best described by each statement.

1. It's a verbal adjective. _____
2. Rome defeated this African city in the Punic Wars. _____
3. African who wrote an autobiography called *Confessiōnēs* (*The Confessions*). _____
4. African city that was the birthplace of an emperor. _____
5. One adjective used to describe the original province of Africa. _____
6. The location of this Roman province in Africa is roughly equivalent to modern Morocco. _____
7. Acronym used to remember Latin adjectives with *-īus* genitive singular endings. _____
8. Roman from Africa who was the author of *Metamorphōsēs* (*The Metamorphoses*), or *Aureus Asinus* (*The Golden Ass*). _____
9. Roman emperor born in Africa. _____
10. Criminal condemned to die in the games. _____

a. Apuleius

b. Augustine

c. Carthage

d. *damnātus*

e. Leptis Magna

f. Mauretania

g. participle

h. *prōconsulāris*

i. Septimius Severus

j. UNUS NAUTA

17-16 *Verba Discenda*: **Meanings.** Select the English equivalent of the Latin word.

1. *alter, altera, alterum* _____
2. *amphitheātrum* _____
3. *carmen* _____
4. *cor* _____
5. *etiam* _____
6. *gladius* _____
7. *ille, illa, illud* _____
8. *ipse* _____
9. *lacrimō* _____
10. *neuter* _____
11. *nullus* _____
12. *numquam* _____
13. *quōmodo* _____
14. *sērius* _____
15. *mūnera* _____
16. *mūnus* _____
17. *tōtus* _____
18. *ullus* _____

a. amphitheater

b. and also, even now

c. any

d. cry, shed tears

e. heart

f. himself, herself, etc.

g. how

h. later, too late

i. neither

j. never

k. none, no

l. obligation

m. poem

n. public games

o. sword

p. that, those

q. the other (of two)

r. whole, all

17-17 Crossword Puzzle. Complete the puzzle with information from the chapter.

Across

3 – The word that starts with "T" in UNUS NAUTA

6 – One of the words starting with "U" in UNUS NAUTA

8 – Rome's bitter African rival

11 – UNUS NAUTA word meaning "another"

12 – UNUS NAUTA word meaning "neither"

13 – _____ (that) *fēmina*

15 – Genitive sing. ending for UNUS NAUTA words

16 – Servilia's favorite poet

17 – *Fēmina* _____ (herself)

18 – Birthplace of St. Augustine

20 – Person condemned to die in the arena games

22 – One of the words starting with "U" in UNUS NAUTA

23 – "Heart"

Down

1 – The word starting with "S" in UNUS NAUTA

2 – "Never"

4 – Emperor born in Africa

5 – "Sword"

7 – Participles show _____ time

9 – He wrote *The Golden Ass*

10 – "Later"

12 – UNUS NAUTA word meaning "none"

14 – "To cry"

19 – "Song, poem"

21 – UNUS NAUTA word meaning "the other"

18 Fugitīvus!

18-01 Perfect or Imperfect? As you read the following story in English, indicate whether the action of the verb would be perfect or imperfect in Latin by selecting the appropriate choice.

Marcus was driving (1) (perfect/imperfect) his chariot along the Via Appia one day. He was listening (2) (perfect/imperfect) to the birds chirping. The sun was shining (3) (perfect/imperfect) brightly. He saw (4) (perfect/imperfect) a man at the side of the road. This man was selling (5) (perfect/imperfect) wine while his wife sang (6) (perfect/imperfect). A dog was sleeping (7) (perfect/imperfect) next to them. Marcus halted (8) (perfect/imperfect) and got out (9) (perfect/imperfect) of his chariot. As Marcus came near, the dog growled (10) (perfect/imperfect). Marcus was scared (11) (perfect/imperfect). He shouted (12) (perfect/imperfect), turned (13) (perfect/imperfect) quickly and remounted (14) (perfect/imperfect) his chariot.

18-02 Imperfect Tense: Forms. Using the formulas given in your textbook for making the imperfect tense, select the form that is a proper imperfect for the verb given.

1. capiō, capere	capēbas	capiēbās
2. habeō, -ēre	habēbat	habiēbat
3. ambulō (1)	ambulēbam	ambulābam
4. dīcō, -ere	dīcēbātis	dīcābātis
5. faciō, -ere	faciēbant	facēbant
6. veniō, -īre	venēbāmus	veniēbāmus

18-03 Translating Imperfects and Perfects. Choose the best English translation for the following Latin verbs.

1. *vocābās*
 a. you were calling **b.** you have called

2. *monēbāmus*
 a. we were warning **b.** we have warned

3. *mōvistis*
 a. you were moving **b.** you have moved

4. *dūcēbant*
 a. they have led **b.** they used to lead

5. *fēcimus*
 a. we used to make **b.** we made

6. *dūcēbās*
 a. you have led **b.** you used to lead

7. *vīdit*
 a. he saw **b.** he used to see

8. *capiēbat*
 a. he was taking **b.** they were taking

9. *audiēbam*
 a. I used to hear **b.** I have heard

10. *cucurristī*
 a. you ran **b.** you were running

18-04 Imperfect Tense: Identification. Select all the verbs in the imperfect tense.

_____ amat		_____ dixī	
_____ amāvit		_____ dīcō	
_____ amābat		_____ capis	
_____ amābit		_____ capiēbas	
_____ vident		_____ cēpistī	
_____ vidēbunt		_____ capiēs	
_____ vīdērunt		_____ dormīmus	
_____ vidēbant		_____ dormīvimus	
_____ dīcam		_____ dormiēbāmus	
_____ dīcēbam		_____ dormient	

18-05 Verb Review: Future. When you learn a new tense it is a good time to review your grasp of all the tenses. Select each verb in the future tense.

_____ amat		_____ dixī	
_____ amāvit		_____ dīcō	
_____ amābat		_____ capis	
_____ amābit		_____ capiēbas	
_____ vident		_____ cēpistī	
_____ vidēbunt		_____ capiēs	
_____ vīdērunt		_____ dormīmus	
_____ vidēbant		_____ dormīvimus	
_____ dīcam		_____ dormiēbāmus	
_____ dīcēbam		_____ dormient	

18-06 Verb Review: Perfect. When you learn a new tense it is a good time to review your grasp of all the tenses. Select each verb in the perfect tense.

_____ amat		_____ dixī	
_____ amāvit		_____ dīcō	
_____ amābat		_____ capis	
_____ amābit		_____ capiēbas	
_____ vident		_____ cēpistī	
_____ vidēbunt		_____ capiēs	
_____ vīdērunt		_____ dormīmus	
_____ vidēbant		_____ dormīvimus	
_____ dīcam		_____ dormiēbāmus	
_____ dīcēbam		_____ dormient	

18-07 Verb Review: Present. When you learn a new tense it is a good time to review your grasp of all the tenses. Select each verb in the present tense.

_____ amat   _____ dixī
_____ amāvit   _____ dīcō
_____ amābat   _____ capis
_____ amābit   _____ capiēbas
_____ vident   _____ cēpistī
_____ vidēbunt   _____ capiēs
_____ vīdērunt   _____ dormīmus
_____ vidēbant   _____ dormīvimus
_____ dīcam   _____ dormiēbāmus
_____ dīcēbam   _____ dormient

18-08 Change the Tense: Present to Imperfect. Change each present tense verb to the same person and number of the imperfect tense. Follow the model.

→ facimus   *faciēbāmus*

1. portātis   _____
2. venit   _____
3. faciunt   _____
4. vidēs   _____
5. dīcō   _____
6. vidēmus   _____

18-09 Four Tense Recognition. Match the Latin word with its English translation.

1. *vocāvit* _____   a. he used to call
2. *vocābat* _____   b. I did
3. *monēbunt* _____   c. I was doing
4. *duxērunt* _____   d. I was seizing
5. *dūcunt* _____   e. I will seize
6. *habēbant* _____   f. she called
7. *habēbunt* _____   g. they are leading
8. *dūcent* _____   h. they led
9. *capiam* _____   i. they used to have
10. *capiēbam* _____   j. they will have
11. *ambulābimus* _____   k. they will lead
12. *ambulābāmus* _____   l. they will warn
13. *dīcis* _____   m. we were walking
14. *dīcēs* _____   n. we will walk
15. *fēcī* _____   o. you say
16. *faciēbam* _____   p. you will say

18-10 Antecedents: English. Select the antecedent for each relative pronoun (who, whose, whom) in the following passage. If an antecedent is repeated, select it each time it appears.

Cordus is the young man whom (1) Servilia loves. But her father has chosen Iullus, an older man whom (2) Servilia dislikes. Servilia, whose (3) best friend lately is her pet bird, does not know how to fight against the customs of her day and asks her brother, to whom (4) she has turned in the past, for help. His advice is for her to make her life with the person who (5) has been chosen for her and to let her father, with whom (6) there is no arguing, alone.

18-11 Relative Pronouns: English. Select the each relative pronoun in the passage below. If the same form is repeated, select it each time it appears. Don't include prepositions, e.g., if the phrase is "of whom," just select "whom."

The slave whom Mendax helps belonged to Zethus. He was searching for his wife, who used to bake bread for Zethus and whom Zethus had sent to another bakery in Calabria. Valeria knew he was a runaway and the name of the man whose slave he was, but all she really saw was a fellow human being to whom she gave some food.

18-12 The Relative Pronoun: *quī, quae, quod*. Complete this chart of *quī, quae, quod*, and use it for the exercises that follow.

	Masculine	Feminine	Neuter
	Singular		
Nominative	quī	quae	quod
Genitive	cuius	1. _____	2. _____
Dative	3. _____	4. _____	cui
Accusative	quem	5. _____	6. _____
Ablative	7. _____	8. _____	quō
	Plural		
Nominative	9. _____	10. _____	11. _____
Genitive	12. _____	13. _____	quōrum
Dative	14. _____	quibus	15. _____
Accusative	16. _____	17. _____	quae
Ablative	quibus	18. _____	quibus

18-13 Relative Pronouns and Antecedents: Gender and Number. Indicate the gender and number of the antecedent (in **bold**) in each sentence. Use masculine and feminine for people, neuter for things. Follow the model.

→ **Bertha** is a woman who is very happy.   *feminine singular*

1. **Bertha** is the woman to whom Fred gave the flowers. _____

2. Fred hit the **man** who had been making a pass at Bertha. _____

3. No one really knows the **man** whose daughter married Fred. _____

4. Watch out for the **women** whose shoes are off! _____

5. The **gifts** that you sent to Bertha have been returned. _____

6. We know the **weapon** with which you disposed of Colonel Fred. _____

7. Show me the **person** who did this to you and I'll fix him! _____

8. These are the **times** that try men's souls. _____

9. The **girls** whom you love are leaving town. _____

10. Fred is following the **girls** who love George. _____

18-14 Relative Pronouns: Case. Indicate what case each relative pronoun (in **bold**) would be in Latin. HINT: If you are unsure, substitute the antecedent for the relative pronoun. Follow the model.

→ Bertha is a woman **who** is very happy.   *nominative*
(Bertha is a woman. Bertha is very happy. This makes it clear that "who" is nominative.)

1. Bertha is the woman **to whom** Fred gave the flowers. _____
2. Fred hit the man **who** had been making a pass at Bertha. _____
3. No one really knows the man **whose** daughter married Fred. _____
4. Watch out for the women **whose** shoes are off! _____
5. The gifts **that** you sent to Bertha have been returned. _____
6. We know the weapon **with which** you disposed of Colonel Fred. _____
7. Show me the person **who** did this to you and I'll fix him! _____
8. These are the times **that** try men's souls. _____
9. The girls **whom** you love are leaving town. _____
10. Fred is following the girls **who** love George. _____

18-15 Relative Pronouns: Latin. Exercises 18-13 and 18-14 prepared you for this one. Select the correct relative pronoun, remembering that the relative pronoun takes its gender and number from the antecedent, but its case from its function in the clause. Follow the model.

→ Bertha is a woman **who** is very happy.
a. quam   **b.** *quae*   **c.** cui   **d.** quem

("Bertha" is nominative and feminine. "Who" is the subject of its clause. Thus: the fem., sing., nom. of the relative pronoun—*quae*)

1. Bertha is the woman **to whom** Fred gave the flowers.
a. quae   **b.** cui   **c.** quem   **d.** quam
2. Fred hit the man **who** had been making a pass at Bertha.
a. quae   **b.** quem   **c.** quī   **d.** cuius
3. No one really knows the man **whose** daughter married Fred.
a. cuius   **b.** cui   **c.** quī   **d.** quem
4. Watch out for the women **whose** shoes are off!
a. cuius   **b.** quibus   **c.** quae   **d.** quārum
5. The gifts **that** you sent to Bertha have been returned.
a. quae   **b.** quōs   **c.** quās   **d.** quibus
6. We know the weapon **with which** you disposed of Colonel Fred.
a. quō   **b.** quā   **c.** quod   **d.** quae
7. Show me the person **who** did this to you and I'll fix him!
a. quī   **b.** quae   **c.** quod   **d.** cui
8. These are the times **that** try men's souls.
a. quī   **b.** quās   **c.** quod   **d.** quae
9. The girls **whom** you love are leaving town.
a. quam   **b.** quae   **c.** quās   **d.** quibus
10. Fred is following the girls **who** love George.
a. quam   **b.** quae   **c.** quās   **d.** quārum

18-16 Relative Pronouns: Choices. Select the relative pronoun that correctly completes each sentence.

1. Licinia et Valeria et Flāvia adveniēbant ad insulam in [quae / quā] habitant.
2. Nōmen ūnī egēnō est Mendax [cui / quō] ōlim nōmen "Quintus" erat.
3. Mendax est vir [quī / quae] pecūniam ab aliīs poscit.
4. Mendax, [quī / quod] nūllam pecūniam habet, cellam propriam invenīre nōn poterat.
5. Mendax spatium [quī / quod] parvum et fētidum, sed siccum, est, habēre poterat.
6. In hōc spatiō habitat Mendax cum fēle suā [cui / quā] Fēlix nōmen est.
7. Haec fēlēs [quem / quae] quinque mūrēs cēpit, in amphitheātrō esse dēbet.
8. Marcus et Lūcius dīcunt dē mūneribus [quae / quōs] vīdērunt.

18-17 Relative Pronouns: English Sentences. Which word is the best choice for the boldface relative pronoun if the sentence were in Latin? Be sure to consider the gender of the antecedent in Latin.

1. The people **who** live in the apartment building like Felix.
   a. quae   **b.** quī   **c.** cui
2. The patrons, **whose** money keeps Valeria in business, like her shop.
   a. cuius   **b.** cui   **c.** quōrum
3. The patrons, **to whom** Valeria renders a fine service, like her shop.
   a. quibus   **b.** cui   **c.** quī
4. The pedagogue **with whom** Lucius goes to school hates monkeys!
   a. cum cuī   **b.** quōcum   **c.** quibuscum
5. Servilia, **who** wants to speak with Cordus, is excited.
   a. quae   **b.** quā   **c.** quam
6. The animals **which** you are buying have a fine pedigree.
   a. quae   **b.** quī   **c.** quōs
7. The gladiator **whom** I trained will fight today in Capua.
   a. quī   **b.** quōs   **c.** quem
8. The family **that** you saw was not mine.
   a. quae   **b.** quem   **c.** quam

18-18 Interrogative Pronouns. Select the form of the interrogative pronoun in each sentence that makes grammatical sense.

1. [Quī / Quōs] ad insulam in Subūrā adveniēbant?
2. [Quibuscum / Quōrum] habitant Aelius et Plōtia?
3. [Quis / Quī] in pistrīnō labōrābat?
4. [Quod / Quid] Mendax Rōmae invenīre nōn poterat?
5. [Quō / Cuius] "domus" sub scālīs est?
6. [Quem / Quī] Valeria salūtat cum in insulam intrat?
7. [Quem / Quā] incolae omnēs amant?
8. [Quid / Quod] Fēlix in insulā capiēbat?
9. [Cui / Quid] Valeria cibum dat?
10. [Quis / Quī] attonitī sunt quod fugitīvus servus est?

18-19 *Verba Discenda.* Match the Latin word with its English meaning.

1. *aliquis, aliquid* ____
2. *almus, -a, -um* ____
3. *brevis, breve* ____
4. *cella, -ae* f. ____
5. *crūdēlis, crūdēle* ____
6. *dominus, -ī* m. ____
7. *emō, emere, ēmī, emptum* ____
8. *fēlix, fēlīcis* ____
9. *incipiō, incipere, incēpī, inceptum* ____
10. *lectus, -ī* m. ____
11. *maestus, -a, -um* ____
12. *nōn sōlum* ____
13. *paene* ____
14. *prīmus, -a, -um* ____
15. *quaerō, quaerere, quaesīvī/quaesiī, quaesītum* ____
16. *quī, quae, quod* ____
17. *quia* ____
18. *quis, quid* ____
19. *uxor, uxōris* f. ____

a. almost
b. ask
c. begin
d. buy
e. couch
f. harsh
g. first
h. lord
i. lucky
j. not only....
k. nourishing
l. room
m. sad
n. short
o. since
p. someone, something
q. who, which, that
r. who? what?
s. wife

18-20 How Closely Did You Read? Match the names and terms with the appropriate description.

1. antecedent ____
2. imperfect ____
3. *instrūmentī genus vōcāle* ____
4. interrogative ____
5. Varro ____
6. Ostia ____
7. relative ____
8. Spartacus ____

a. the Latin tense expressing a continuous past action
b. a pronoun or adjective that asks a question
c. a pronoun or adjective that connects or relates two pieces of information
d. a Thracian gladiator who led a slave revolt
e. the port of ancient Rome
f. the author of a book called *Dē Rē Rusticā* (On Country Matters)
g. a definition of a slave
h. the word with which a relative pronoun agrees in gender and number

18-21 Crossword Puzzle. Complete the puzzle using information from the chapter.

Across

3 – Huge farms owned by wealthy Romans

5 – Led slave rebellion

7 – "Short animal" _____ *animal*

9 – "Almost"

12 – "To begin"

16 – "Cui"

18 – The word to which a relative pronoun refers in a sentence

20 – Emperor who expanded Ostia

21 – "Quam"

22 – "Whose" (masc. pl.)

25 – "Cruel"

26 – "We were"

27 – *Quid prō* _____

Down

1 – _____ Mater

2 – "Maestus"

4 – Rome's port

6 – Beggar's cat

7 – Tense marker for the imperfect tense

8 – *Non solum... sed* _____

10 – "Y'all were"

11 – "Couch, bed"

13 – Beggar in our story

14 – Name of the runaway's master

15 – The animals (that) I own. What is "that" in Latin?

17 – "Cuius"

19 – Abbreviation on a runaway's collar

20 – _____ *bonō?*

23 – "BWIOF whom" (pl.)

24 – Wrote *Dē Rē Rusticā*

19 Vēnātiō

19-01 Formula for the Pluperfect. Fill in the blanks with words from the *Thēsaurus Verbōrum*. Not every word is used, and none is used twice.

Thēsaurus Verbōrum

1ˢᵗ	*-istis*
2ⁿᵈ	*-erant*
3ʳᵈ	*-ērunt*
-erās	*-ī*
-erat	*-ō*
-erit	perfect
-erāmus	present
-erimus	*-re*
-erātis	short present

To form the pluperfect tense, take the (1) _____ stem, which is found by dropping the
(2) _____ from the (3) _____ principal part, and add the endings

-eram   (6) _____

(4) _____   (7) _____

(5) _____   (8) _____

19-02 Pluperfect Tense. Match the pluperfect with its English translation.

1. *amāverat* _____
2. *audīveram* _____
3. *cucurrerant* _____
4. *dixerās* _____
5. *fueram* _____
6. *māluerātis* _____
7. *nōluerās* _____
8. *potuerant* _____
9. *vēnerat* _____
10. *vīcerant* _____
11. *vīderāmus* _____
12. *voluerant* _____

a. he had come
b. he had loved
c. I had been
d. I had heard
e. they had run
f. they had wanted
g. we had seen
h. they had been able
i. you had not wanted
j. you had preferred
k. you had said
l. they had conquered

19-03 Verb Review: Pluperfect. Select all the verbs in the pluperfect tense.

_____ amat		_____ dixī	
_____ amāvit		_____ dixeram	
_____ amāverat		_____ erat	
_____ amābat		_____ capis	
_____ amābit		_____ cēperat	
_____ vident		_____ capiēbas	
_____ vidēbunt		_____ potuerat	
_____ vīderant		_____ erāmus	
_____ vīdērunt		_____ dormīmus	
_____ poterās		_____ dormīvimus	
_____ dīcam		_____ fuerāmus	
_____ dīcēbam		_____ dormīverāmus	

19-04 The Pluperfect Tense. Select the Latin pluperfect that translates the English verbs.

1. they had replied
  a. *responderant*   **b.** *respondērunt*   **c.** *respondent*   **d.** *respondēbant*

2. I had come
  a. *vēnī*   **b.** *vēneram*   **c.** *veniam*   **d.** *veniēbam*

3. you had conquered
  a. *vincitis*   **b.** *vincēbātis*   **c.** *vīcerātis*   **d.** *vīcistis*

4. you had seen
  a. *vīdistī*   **b.** *vīderās*   **c.** *vidēs*   **d.** *vidēbās*

5. we had wished
  a. *voluerāmus*   **b.** *volumus*   **c.** *volēbāmus*   **d.** *voluimus*

6. they had been
  a. *erant*   **b.** *fuērunt*   **c.** *fuerant*   **d.** *erunt*

19-05 Mixed Tenses. Select the correct Latin translation for each of the following English verbal phrases.

1. they fled
  a. *fūgerant*   **b.** *fūgērunt*   **c.** *fugiunt*   **d.** *fugiēbant*

2. they had fled
  a. *fūgerant*   **b.** *fūgērunt*   **c.** *fugiunt*   **d.** *fugiēbant*

3. they will flee
  a. *fūgerant*   **b.** *fūgērunt*   **c.** *fugiunt*   **d.** *fugient*

4. they were fleeing
  a. *fūgerant*   **b.** *fūgērunt*   **c.** *fugiunt*   **d.** *fugiēbant*

5. they are fleeing
  a. *fūgerant*   **b.** *fūgērunt*   **c.** *fugiunt*   **d.** *fugient*

6. I was able
  a. *potuī*   **b.** *poterō*   **c.** *potueram*   **d.** *possum*

7. they had been
  a. *fuērunt*   **b.** *erant*   **c.** *erunt*   **d.** *fuerant*

8. I have been
  a. *fueram*   **b.** *fuī*   **c.** *eram*   **d.** *sum*

19-06 The Demonstrative *hic, haec, hoc*. Select the form of *hic, haec, hoc* that agrees with the word marked in **bold** in each sentence.

1. [Hic / Haec] **servus** iēiūnus est.

2. Mendax [huic / huius] **fugitīvō** auxilium dat.

3. Fēminae ad [hunc / hanc] **fugitīvum** pecūniam mittunt.

4. [Huius / Hōrum] **virī** filius ad Forum ībat.

5. [Hae / Haec] **vōcēs** dulcēs sunt.

6. Multī hominēs [haec / hae] **mūnera** vīdērunt.

7. Mūnera in [hōc / hāc] **terrā** pulchra sunt.

8. Marcus [hōs / hīs] **hominēs** vīdit.

9. Puer [huic / hīs] **animālibus** nōmina dedit.

10. [Hic / Hoc] **imperātor** populō mūnera dabit.

19-07 The Demonstrative *hic, haec, hoc* as a Substantive. The demonstrative *hic, haec, hoc* is very often used as a substantive. Select the form that best translates the words marked in **bold** in each sentence. Keep gender in mind. Follow the model.

→ Give the bread **to this man**.
   a. *hunc*   **b.** huius   **c.** *huic*

1. I am the maid servant **of this woman**.
   a. hārum   **b.** hae   **c.** huius

2. The woman gave assistance **to these men**.
   a. hōrum   **b.** huic   **c.** hīs

3. **These things** are difficult to do.
   a. hoc   **b.** haec   **c.** hae

4. I am looking for **this man**.
   a. hunc   **b.** hanc   **c.** huic

5. **This man's** son is smart.
   a. huius   **b.** huic   **c.** hunc

6. **These men's** business is stronger than theirs.
   a. huius   **b.** huic   **c.** hōrum

19-08 Comparatives: Formation. Select the correct comparative of the given adjective. Watch out for irregular comparative forms!

1. maestus, -a, -um	maestior	maesterior
2. līber, -era, -erum	līberior	lībrior
3. parvus, -a, -um	minor	parvior
4. pulcher, -chra, -chrum	pulcherior	pulchrior
5. bonus, -a, -um	bonior	melior
6. laetus, -a, -um	laeterior	laetior
7. malus, -a, -um	melior	pēior
8. magnus, -a, -um	minor	māior
9. cārus, -a, -um	cārior	cārerior
10. multī	plūs	plūrēs

19-09 GNC'ing! Comparative Adjectives. Select the correct GNC for these noun and comparative adjective pairs.

1. animālia minōra
   a. nom. sing.   b. acc. pl.   c. abl. sing.

2. fēminae minōris
   a. nom. pl.   b. gen. sing.   c. dat. sing.

3. fēminae minōrī
   a. nom. pl.   b. gen. sing.   c. dat. sing.

4. fēminae minōrēs
   a. nom. pl.   b. gen. sing.   c. dat. sing.

5. nautae māiōrēs
   a. nom. pl.   b. gen. sing.   c. dat. sing.

6. puellīs pulchriōrībus
   a. acc. pl.   b. gen. sing.   c. dat. pl.

7. puerōrum maestiōrum
   a. acc. sing.   b. acc. pl.   c. gen. pl.

8. puerō laetiore
   a. dat. sing.   b. abl. sing   c. acc. pl.

19-10 Comparative Adjectives: English to Latin. Select the correct Latin for the English noun and comparative adjective pairs in **bold**.

1. This food is **for the smaller gladiator**.
   a. gladiātōre minōre   b. gladiātōrī minōrī   c. gladiātor minor

2. **The swifter gladiators** get the trophy.
   a. gladiātōrēs celeriōrī   b. gladiātōrēs celeriōrae   c. gladiātōrēs celeriōrēs

3. I am watching **the wearier maid servants**. They need a break.
   a. fessiōrem ancillam   b. fessiōrēs ancilla   c. fessiōrēs ancillās

4. I want the names **of the larger students**.
   a. discipulī māiōris   b. discipulōrum māiōrum   c. discipulōrum māiōrium

5. Give the the best oats **to the faster horses**.
   a. celeriōribus equīs   b. celeriōrī equō   c. celeriōris equī

6. **Luckier men** than I have died in the arena.
   a. virēs fēliciōrōs   b. virī fēliciōrī   c. virī fēliciōrēs

19-17 *Verba Discenda:* **Meanings.** Match the Latin word with its English meaning.

1. *abdō, abdere, abdidī, abditum* _____   **a.** against
2. *absum, abesse, āfuī* _____   **b.** altar
3. *āra, -ae* f. _____   **c.** be gone
4. *contrā* (+ acc.) _____   **d.** before
5. *cōtīdiē* _____   **e.** better
6. *grātia, -ae* f. _____   **f.** daily
7. *heri* _____   **g.** former
8. *hic, haec, hoc* _____   **h.** grace
9. *inspectō* (1) _____   **i.** hide
10. *locus, -ī* m. _____   **j.** higher
11. *longus, -a, -um* _____   **k.** long
12. *melior, melius* _____   **l.** look closely at
13. *minor, minus* _____   **m.** more (in number)
14. *ōlim* _____   **n.** once
15. *pars, partis* f. _____   **o.** piece
16. *pēior, pēius* _____   **p.** place
17. *plūrēs, plūra* _____   **q.** smaller
18. *prior, prius* _____   **r.** this
19. *priusquam* _____   **s.** worse
20. *superior, superius* _____   **t.** yesterday

19-18 **How Closely Did You Read?** Match the phrase or description to the term it describes.

1. A gladiator lightly armed with a helmet, greaves on both legs, an arm guard (*manica, -ae* f.), a small shield (*parmula, -ae* f.), and a short sword (*sīca, -ae* f.) _____
2. A gladiator lightly armed with a net and a trident _____
3. A heavily armed and armored gladiator equipped with helmet (*galea, -ae* f.), oblong shield (*scūtum, -ī* n.), sword (*gladius, -iī* m.), wide leather belt (*balteus, -eī* m.), and metal greave (*ōcrea, -ae* f.) _____
4. A heavily armed gladiator who wore a special, fish-shaped helmet _____
5. Latin motto on the Great Seal of the United States _____
6. This tense is translated with the English helping verb "had" _____
7. Adding *-ior* to many adjectives makes them this _____
8. Animal fighter _____
9. Gladiatorial school located adjacent to the Flavian Amphitheater _____
10. Statue located next to the Flavian Amphitheater _____
11. Roman poet who wrote about a gladiator named Hermes _____
12. Latin salute of Roman gladiators _____
13. The Latin motto of the International Olympic Games _____
14. The real name of the Colosseum _____

a. *Avē imperātor. Moritūrī tē salūtant!*   e. comparative   j. mirmillo
b. *bestiārius*   f. *Ē pluribus ūnum*   k. pluperfect
c. *Citius, altius, fortius*   g. Flavian Amphitheater   l. *rētiārius*
d. Colossus of Nero   h. Ludus Magnus   m. samnite
                                               i. Martial   n. *thrāx*

19-19 Crossword Puzzle. Complete the puzzle with information from the chapter.

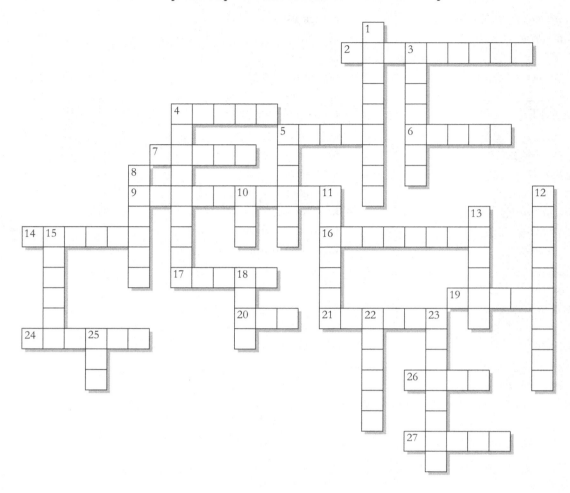

Across

2 – Emperor who began the Flavian Amphitheater
4 – "Worse"
5 – "Bigger, older"
6 – Pluperfect ending: "they had ..."
7 – Emperor who finished the Flavian Amphitheater
9 – Fighter against animals
14 – *Lūdus* _____; Rome's premier gladiatorial school
16 – Gladiator wearing a fish shaped helmet
17 – "Smaller"
19 – "Former"
20 – Genitive singular ending of both *hic* and *ille*
21 – Pluperfect ending: "we had ..."
24 – Owned the runaway slave
26 – "Yesterday"
27 – "Place"

Down

1 – Gladiator armed with a net
3 – Stem used to form pluperfect tense
4 – "Before"
5 – "Better"
8 – "To be gone"
10 – "Altar"
11 – Most heavily armed gladiator
12 – The ablative of _____ is translated "than"
13 – "Against"
15 – "To conceal"
18 – "Once, formerly"
22 – "To be there for someone"
23 – "Higher"
25 – Helping verb used to translate the pluperfect

20   Nōn Perseus sed Herculēs!

20-01 Forming Superlatives. Choose the masculine nominative singular, superlative form of each adjective.

1. laetus, -a, -um   laetimus   laetissimus
2. īrātus, -a, -um   īrātior   īrātissimus
3. miser, -a, -um   miserrissimus   miserrimus
4. cārus, -a, -um   cārissimus   cārimus
5. bonus, -a, -um   bonissimus   optimus
6. malus, -a, -um   pessimus   malissimus
7. similis, -e   simillimus   similissimus
8. facilis, -e   facilissimus   facillimus
9. pulcher, -chra, -chrum   pulchrissimus   pulcherrimus
10. magnus, -a, -um   magnissimus   maximus

20-02 Superlatives: All Cases. Choose the correct superlative form for each adjective. Keep the GNC the same.

1. laetus
   a. laetissimus   **b.** laetissima   **c.** laetissimum   **d.** laetissimae
2. fortis
   a. fortissimus   **b.** fortissimum   **c.** fortissimis   **d.** fortissimō
3. miser
   a. miserrimum   **b.** miserius   **c.** miserissimus   **d.** miserrimus
4. pulchra
   a. pulcherissima   **b.** pulcherrima   **c.** pulcherrimus   **d.** pulchrius
5. ācer
   a. ācerissima   **b.** ācerrima   **c.** ācerrimus   **d.** ācerissimus
6. facilior
   a. facilissimus   **b.** facillimus   **c.** faciliorissimus   **d.** facillimum
7. difficilius
   a. difficilissimum   **b.** difficiliorissimum **c.** difficillimum   **d.** difficillimus
8. similēs
   a. simillimās   **b.** simillima   **c.** simillissimōs   **d.** simillimibus

20-03 Irregular Superlatives. Match the adjective with its superlative.

1. bonus _____   **a.** optimus
2. magnus _____   **b.** pessimus
3. malus _____   **c.** maximus
4. multus _____   **d.** minimus
5. parvus _____   **e.** plurimus
6. superus _____   **f.** suprēmus

20-04 Comparatives and Superlatives: Review. Match the comparative with its superlative.

1. māior _____   **a.** optimus
2. melior _____   **b.** pessimus
3. minor _____   **c.** maximus
4. pēior _____   **d.** minimus
5. plūrēs _____   **e.** plūrimī
6. superior _____   **f.** suprēmus

20-05 Comparatives and Superlatives: Derivatives. Use your knowledge of the irregular comparatives and superlatives to match the meaning of the English word with its definition.

1. pejorative _____   **a.** having a worse than negative overtone
2. ameliorate _____   **b.** inferior in importance
3. pessimist _____   **c.** the act of making the best of something
4. optimist _____   **d.** one who believes the worst will happen
5. optimization _____   **e.** one who hopes for the best
6. majority _____   **f.** the best possible
7. minor _____   **g.** the bigger portion
8. maximize _____   **h.** the least possible
9. minimal _____   **i.** to increase as much as possible
10. optimal _____   **j.** to make better

20-06 Comparatives and Superlatives: Derivatives in Context. Each of the English words marked in **bold** is derived from a Latin comparative or superlative. Supply each comparative or superlative by filling the blank. Follow the model.

Charley was in an **optimistic** ⟶ *optimus, -a, -um* mood when he **minimized** (1)_____ his computer screen, stood up, and strode into the meeting. Here he hoped to **maximize** (2)_____the company's profits by swaying a **majority** (3)_____of the shareholders and winning a **plurality** (4)_____ of the voters. First, though, he would have to explain a **pejorative** (5)_____ remark about the CEO and his **prior** (6) _____ statements about a **pessimistic** (7) _____financial future for the country.

20-07 Translating *Quam*. Select the correct translation for the words in **bold**.

1. Soror mea **māior quam** frāter meus est.
   a. bigger than   **b.** as big as possible

2. Currō **melius quam** tū.
   a. better than   **b.** as well as possible.

3. Labōrā **quam strēnuissimē**!
   a. harder than   **b.** as hard as possible

4. Hic liber **pēior quam** ille est.
   a. worse than   **b.** as bad as possible

5. Ille adulescens **quam celerrimē** currit.
   a. faster than   **b.** as fast as possible

6. Nēmō **almior quam** Valeria est!
   a. kinder than   **b.** as kind as possible

20-08 Comprehension: *Lectiō Prīma*. Find the Latin words in *Lectiō Prīma* that answer each question. Translate these words. The number of the line(s) where you will find the answer is given in parentheses. Follow the model.

→ At what time of day does this *lectiō* take place? (line 1) *nocte,* at night

1. What does Licinia say about her feelings concerning the prediction the astrologer made about her baby? (line 4) _____

2. How does Aelius react to his wife's feelings? (line 7) _____

3. What command does Aelius give his wife? (lines 7–8) _____

4. To what hero does Aelius compare his son? (line 9) _____

5. Who does Aelius believe will protect his son? (line 12) _____

6. Whom did the goddess Juno hate? (line 17) _____

7. What does she send to the family? (line 18) _____

8. Where do Hercules and his brother sleep? (lines 20–21) _____

9. How does Iphicles, Hercules' brother, respond to the danger? (line 24) _____

10. What does Hercules show? (line 30) _____

20-09 Future Perfect Tense: Formation. Complete the formula for forming the future perfect tense by filling in the blanks. Use words from the *Thēsaurus Verbōrum*. Not every word is used, and none is used twice.

Thēsaurus Verbōrum

1st	-eris
2nd	-erunt
3rd	-ī
-erāmus	-ō
-erant	perfect
-erās	present
-erimus	-re
-erint	short present

To form the future perfect tense, take the (1) _____ stem, which is formed by taking the (2) _____ PP and dropping the (3) _____ from it. To this stem add the endings:

-erō   (5) _____

(4) _____   -eritis

-erit   (6) _____

20-10 Perfect System Tenses: Identification and Review.
When you learn a new tense, it is also time to review the ones you already know. Identify the tense of the following verbs. Be careful of false indicators!

1. *vocāvit*
   a. perfect   b. pluperfect   c. future perfect

2. *vocāverat*
   a. perfect   b. pluperfect   c. future perfect

3. *duxeram*
   a. perfect   b. pluperfect   c. future perfect

4. *duxerō*
   a. perfect   b. pluperfect   c. future perfect

5. *duxit*
   a. perfect   b. pluperfect   c. future perfect

6. *vīcistī*
   a. perfect   b. pluperfect   c. future perfect

7. *vīceritis*
   a. perfect   b. pluperfect   c. future perfect

8. *vīcerātis*
   a. perfect   b. pluperfect   c. future perfect

9. *potuerās*
   a. perfect   b. pluperfect   c. future perfect

10. *voluerit*
   a. perfect   b. pluperfect   c. future perfect

20-11 Tricky Verbs: Tense Identification.
Some verbs can fool you if you do not consider their stem carefully. This is especially true for certain irregular verbs. When in doubt, check the stem!

1. *erat*
   a. pluperfect   b. perfect   c. pluperfect   d. imperfect

2. *fuerit*
   a. future   b. pluperfect   c. future perfect   d. imperfect

3. *fuerat*
   a. pluperfect   b. future perfect   c. imperfect   d. present

4. *poterō*
   a. future   b. future perfect   c. present   d. perfect

5. *eris*
   a. future   b. future perfect   c. imperfect   d. pluperfect

6. *potuerimus*
   a. future   b. future perfect   c. imperfect   d. perfect

7. *potuit*
   a. perfect   b. present   c. future perfect   d. pluperfect

8. *potuimus*
   a. future   b. future perfect   c. imperfect   d. perfect

9. *potes*
   a. future   b. perfect   c. present   d. imperfect

10. *voluistī*
   a. present   b. future   c. perfect   d. pluperfect

20-12 Perfect System: Endings. Without changing the person and number of the verb, complete the chart with the correct perfect, pluperfect, and future perfect endings to match the person and number row by row. The stem is provided. Follow the model.

	Perfect	Pluperfect	Future Perfect
Sing.			
1st	→ salutāvī	salutāveram	salutāverō
2nd	salutāvistī	1. salutāv_____	2. salutāv_____
3rd	3. salutāv_____	salutāverat	4. salutāv_____
Pl.			
1st	5. salutāv_____	salutāverāmus	6. salutāv_____
2nd	7. salutāv_____	8. salutāv_____	salutāveritis
3rd	salutāvērunt	9. salutāv_____	10. salutāv_____

20-13 All Verbs: Translation, Latin to English. Select the correct answer for the given form. Be careful of false indicators! HINT: The person and number are the same for each set of forms. Only the tense changes.

1. *vēneris*
  a. you will come   **b.** you come   **c.** you will have come   **d.** you came

2. *scripserant*
  a. they wrote   **b.** they will have written   **c.** they will write   **d.** they had written

3. *ambulāvit*
  a. he had walked   **b.** he walked   **c.** he will walk   **d.** he will have walked

4. *ambulābit*
  a. he will walk   **b.** he had walked   **c.** he walked   **d.** he will have walked

5. *vidēs*
  a. you saw   **b.** you see   **c.** you will have seen   **d.** you will see

6. *mittēmus*
  a. we will send   **b.** we will have sent   **c.** we send   **d.** we were sending

7. *exspectāvimus*
  a. we had expected   **b.** we have expected   **c.** we expect   **d.** we will have expected

8. *incēperit*
  a. she will begin   **b.** she was beginning   **c.** she will have begun   **d.** she had begun

20-14 Verb Translation Review: English to Latin. Select the Latin that corresponds to the English verb phrase.

1. she had bought
  a. *emit*   **b.** *ēmerat*   **c.** *emet*   **d.** *ēmit*

2. you will find
  a. *inveniēs*   **b.** *inveniēbās*   **c.** *invēnerās*   **d.** *invēnistī*

3. we found
  a. *invēnimus*   **b.** *invēnerāmus*   **c.** *invenimus*   **d.** *invēnerimus*

4. he was coming
  a. *vēnerat*   **b.** *vēnit*   **c.** *venit*   **d.** *veniēbat*

5. I was able
  a. *poterō*   **b.** *poteram*   **c.** *potuerō*   **d.** *potueram*

6. y'all have been
- **a.** *fuerātis*
- **b.** *fuistis*
- **c.** *fueritis*
- **d.** *erātis*

7. I had been able
- **a.** *poterō*
- **b.** *poteram*
- **c.** *potuī*
- **d.** *potueram*

8. she has come
- **a.** *advenit*
- **b.** *advēnerat*
- **c.** *advēnit*
- **d.** *advēnerit*

9. you are fleeing
- **a.** *fūgistī*
- **b.** *fūgerās*
- **c.** *fugis*
- **d.** *fugiēs*

10. I used to walk
- **a.** *ambulābō*
- **b.** *ambulāvī*
- **c.** *ambulāverō*
- **d.** *ambulābam*

20-15 **All Verbs: Present Tense.** Using the principal parts of the verbs in the *Thēsaurus Verbōrum*, select all the present tense forms.

Thēsaurus Verbōrum

ambulō (1)
videō, vidēre, vīdī
iaciō, iacere, iēcī
vincō, vincere, vīcī
audiō, -īre, -īvī

_____ ambulābat	_____ audīvistis	_____ vidēmus
_____ ambulābit	_____ audīverint	_____ vīderās
_____ ambulant	_____ iaciēs	_____ vīderit
_____ ambulāverat	_____ iēcerātis	_____ vīdistī
_____ ambulāveritis	_____ iacis	_____ vincēbant
_____ ambulāvērunt	_____ iēceris	_____ vincēmus
_____ audiam	_____ iēcimus	_____ vīcerant
_____ audīs	_____ iaciēbam	_____ vincunt
_____ audiēbās	_____ vidēbās	_____ vīcī
_____ audīverātis	_____ vidēbimus	_____ vīcerō

20-16 All Verbs: Future Tense. Using the principal parts of the verbs in the *Thēsaurus Verbōrum*, select all the future tense forms.

Thēsaurus Verbōrum

ambulō (1)
videō, vidēre, vīdī
iaciō, iacere, iēcī
vincō, vincere, vīcī
audiō, -īre, -īvī

_____ ambulābat	_____ audīvistis	_____ vidēbimus
_____ ambulābit	_____ audīverint	_____ vidēmus
_____ ambulant	_____ iaciēs	_____ viderās
_____ ambulāverat	_____ iēcerātis	_____ vīderit
_____ ambulāveritis	_____ iacis	_____ vīdistī
_____ ambulāvērunt	_____ iēceris	_____ vincēbant
_____ audiam	_____ iēcimus	_____ vincēmus
_____ audīs	_____ iaciēbam	_____ vincunt
_____ audiēbās	_____ vīcerant	_____ vīcī
_____ audīverātis	_____ vidēbās	_____ vīcerō

20-17 All Verbs: Imperfect Tense. Using the principal parts of the verbs in the *Thēsaurus Verbōrum*, select all the imperfect tense forms.

Thēsaurus Verbōrum

ambulō (1)
videō, vidēre, vīdī
iaciō, iacere, iēcī
vincō, vincere, vīcī
audiō, -īre, -īvī

_____ ambulābat	_____ audīvistis	_____ vidēmus
_____ ambulābit	_____ audīverint	_____ viderās
_____ ambulant	_____ iaciēs	_____ vīderit
_____ ambulāverat	_____ iēcerātis	_____ vīdistī
_____ ambulāveritis	_____ iacis	_____ vincēbant
_____ ambulāvērunt	_____ iēceris	_____ vincēmus
_____ audiam	_____ iaciēbam	_____ vīcerant
_____ audīs	_____ iēcimus	_____ vincunt
_____ audīverātis	_____ vidēbās	_____ vīcī
_____ audiēbās	_____ vidēbimus	_____ vīcerō

20-18 All Verbs: Perfect Tense. Using the principal parts of the verbs in the *Thēsaurus Verbōrum*, select all the perfect tense forms.

Thēsaurus Verbōrum

ambulō (1)
videō, vidēre, vīdī
iaciō, iacere, iēcī
vincō, vincere, vīcī
audiō, -īre, -īvī

_____ ambulābat	_____ audīvistis	_____ vidēmus
_____ ambulābit	_____ audīverint	_____ vīderās
_____ ambulant	_____ iaciēs	_____ vīderit
_____ ambulāverat	_____ iēcerātis	_____ vīdistī
_____ ambulāveritis	_____ iacis	_____ vincēbant
_____ ambulāvērunt	_____ iēceris	_____ vincēmus
_____ audiam	_____ iēcimus	_____ vīcerant
_____ audīs	_____ iaciēbam	_____ vincunt
_____ audīverātis	_____ vidēbās	_____ vīcī
_____ audiēbās	_____ vidēbimus	_____ vīcerō

20-19 All Verbs: Pluperfect Tense. Using the principal parts of the verbs in the *Thēsaurus Verbōrum*, select all the pluperfect tense forms.

Thēsaurus Verbōrum

ambulō (1)
videō, vidēre, vīdī
iaciō, iacere, iēcī
vincō, vincere, vīcī
audiō, -īre, -īvī

_____ ambulābat	_____ audīvistis	_____ vidēmus
_____ ambulābit	_____ audīverint	_____ vīderās
_____ ambulant	_____ iaciēs	_____ vīderit
_____ ambulāverat	_____ iacis	_____ vīdistī
_____ ambulāveritis	_____ iēcerātis	_____ vincēbant
_____ ambulāvērunt	_____ iēceris	_____ vincēmus
_____ audiam	_____ iēcimus	_____ vīcerant
_____ audīs	_____ iaciēbam	_____ vincunt
_____ audīverātis	_____ vidēbās	_____ vīcī
_____ audiēbās	_____ vidēbimus	_____ vīcerō

20-20 All Verbs: Future Perfect. Using the principal parts of the verbs in the *Thēsaurus Verbōrum*, select all the future perfect tense forms.

Thēsaurus Verbōrum

ambulō (1)
videō, vidēre, vīdī
iaciō, iacere, iēcī
vincō, vincere, vīcī
audiō, -īre, -īvī

_____ ambulābat	_____ audiēbās	_____ vidēmus
_____ ambulābit	_____ audīverint	_____ viderās
_____ ambulant	_____ iaciēs	_____ vīderit
_____ ambulāverat	_____ iēcerātis	_____ vīdistī
_____ ambulāveritis	_____ iacis	_____ vincēbant
_____ ambulāvērunt	_____ iēceris	_____ vincēmus
_____ audiam	_____ iēcimus	_____ vincunt
_____ audīs	_____ iaciēbam	_____ vīcī
_____ audīverātis	_____ vidēbās	_____ vīcerō
_____ audīvistis	_____ vidēbimus	

20-21 How Closely Did You Read? Match the name or term that is best identified by each statement.

1. The mother of Hercules. _____
2. The wife of Hercules. _____
3. Hercules' stepmother. _____
4. A temple of Hercules is located here. _____
5. Strangled snakes when just an infant. _____
6. This kind of word means "as … as possible" when used with *quam*. _____
7. A monster Hercules defeated. _____
8. This tense is used to show an action that "will have happened" before another action._____

a. Alcmena
b. Cacus
c. Forum Boarium
d. future perfect
e. Hercules
f. Juno
g. Megara
h. superlative

20-22 Crossword Puzzle. Complete the puzzle with information from the chapter.

Across

1 – "Worse"

3 – "Immediately"

5 – "Smaller"

6 – "Shout"

7 – Site of the oracle Hercules consulted

8 – The Forum ____

10 – "To send"

12 – "Deed"

14 – "Worst"

16 – "However"

18 – "Bigger"

19 – "Smallest"

21 – King who ordered Hercules's labors

23 – Roman monster defeated by Hercules

24 – "Easy"

Down

1 – Name of the oracular priestess at Delphi

2 – *Orbis* ____, the world

3 – "Highest"

4 – "Finally"

5 – "Better"

9 – "Best"

11 – "Then"

13 – "But"

15 – "For, because"

17 – "Biggest"

20 – Wife whom Hercules kills

22 – "Crime"